# Genesis from Scratch

Also from Westminster John Knox Press by Donald L. Griggs

*The Bible from Scratch: The Old Testament for Beginners*
*The Bible from Scratch: The New Testament for Beginners*
*Mark's Gospel from Scratch: The New Testament for Beginners* (with Charles
    D. Myers Jr.)

# Genesis from Scratch

*The Old Testament for Beginners*

## Donald L. Griggs
## W. Eugene March

WJK WESTMINSTER JOHN KNOX PRESS
LOUISVILLE • KENTUCKY

*First edition*
Published by Westminster John Knox Press
Louisville, Kentucky

10 11 12 13 14 15 16 17 18 19—10 9 8 7 6 5 4 3 2 1

*Book design by Teri Kays Vinson*
*Cover design by Night & Day Design*

**Library of Congress Cataloging-in-Publication Data**

Griggs, Donald L.
    Genesis from scratch : the Old Testament for beginners / Donald L.
Griggs, W. Eugene March.
        p. cm.
    Includes bibliographical references (p.        ).
    ISBN 978-0-664-23507-9 (alk. paper)
    1. Bible. O.T. Genesis—Textbooks. 2. Bible O.T.—Study and teaching.
I. March, W. Eugene (Wallace Eugene), 1935- II. Title.
    BS1239.G74 2010
    222'.11061071—dc22

                                                            2009040195

PRINTED IN THE UNITED STATES OF AMERICA

♾ The paper used in this publication meets the minimum requirements of the American National Standard for Information Sciences—Permanence of Paper for Printed Library Materials, ANSI Z39.48-1992

Westminster John Knox Press advocates the responsible use of our natural resources. The text paper of this book is made from 30% post-consumer waste.

# Contents

*Part One*

# PARTICIPANT'S GUIDE

**W. EUGENE MARCH**

# Preface to Part One

Well-known stories, numerous glimpses of life in the ancient Middle East, drama, humor, poignant grief—all are to be found in the book of Genesis, and all are what have long drawn me to this book!

Genesis has a long history of development. Much of the material was passed orally from generation to generation for several hundreds of years before it was written down. These originally separate traditions were then crafted together in the midst of severe crisis situations and provided a narrative framework. The details of some stories reflect social custom and legal practice that clearly place them in Mesopotamia or in Egypt in the middle of the second millennium BCE. Others stem from a period some six hundred years later. The puzzle of the development of Genesis continues to engage readers.

There is something else that has always attracted me to Genesis: its literary quality and its insight into the human condition. There are numerous interesting and well-told stories that capture the imagination and touch the common humanity that we all share. They address such basic human concerns as "Why are we here?" and "How can siblings live together productively and peaceably?" Issues of human choice and divine providence are explored. Insight is offered into the nature of God and the divine relationship with humankind. And all of these stories are presented with the people of the world as the intended audience. Yes, a particular people called "Israel" will emerge with a special role, but Genesis is about God's concern for *all* of us, and not just one particular people. These stories from long ago still have good insights to offer us about the world in which we live.

As I approached this study, I focused on three major matters of concern. First, there was the size of Genesis. There is a lot here! How could I provide a good, representative taste of such a huge and delicious morsel? Second, I considered how to provide enough historical and linguistic background to help the reader without becoming pedantic or violating the literary integrity of the various accounts. As with most things, the more one knows about a subject, the deeper one's appreciation of its delights and pitfalls. This background information is critical. And third, I pondered the best ways to indicate how I read Genesis (as well as other parts of the Bible) as a very human document that God continues to use to address me and my life situation.

In connection with the first concern I tried to pick some parts of Genesis that I think are the most important and interesting. The sections that I chose are important because they provide key insight into the overall purpose of Genesis. While there is much that is not considered in this study, the basic story line and primary people are presented. I have tried to allow the reader to gain an appreciation for the way the stories are developed literarily as well as theologically. Where I thought it might be particularly helpful, I have referenced the original language of the text and suggested ways that different translations have chosen to "interpret" the tradition. Likewise with archaeological data, where I thought it could be useful I have tried to include a little.

The matter of how the Bible—in this case Genesis—continues to be a source of divine guidance for me was more difficult to address. I have not provided any sort of "systematic" or "dogmatic" treatment of biblical authority. But, for me personally, the Bible does have an "authority" that I do not ascribe to other literature. I don't try to argue about it, but I assume it. Thus, when I read a biblical passage, one part of me seeks to understand how what I am studying offers me insight into myself or suggestions about how to deal with decisions that are before me. I believe that careful study of the Bible can help me mature and have a better relationship with God, with people close to me, and with humankind more broadly. While I fully enjoy the human literary character of the Bible with all of its drama, I read it with a different set of expectations than those I take to most other literature. My presentations will no doubt reveal some of my bias.

There are several ways I hope you as a reader/participant in this course will benefit. First, I hope that you will be grasped by the sheer beauty and power of Genesis. It is such an interesting and thought-provoking piece of literature! Second, I hope you will discover the treasure that a careful study of a biblical text can uncover. To read and reread a passage, to explore the meaning of particular words and phrases, to enter the world of the text imaginatively—all these steps can assist in gaining a clearer and deeper appreciation of the Bible and of any other literature. Third, I hope this study will provide more than simply intellectual stimulation, though I certainly hope that happens as well. But the broader goal of Bible study is to draw the reader/participant into the biblical world and into life with people who continue to cherish this book. This rather diverse company includes a variety of Christians, Jews, and Muslims as well as some people who simply find the Bible a "must" read for a full experience of life.

Read and listen carefully to Genesis, for I am convinced that there is great reward to be found. Have a good study!

Louisville, Kentucky
June 2009

# *Chapter One*

# Beginnings

## *A Study of Genesis 1:1–2:25; 6:1–22; 9:1–17*

## Introduction

Memorable writings usually have noteworthy beginnings. You get a clue about where you are going, but only hints, not the full story. So it is with the Bible! Genesis is the name of the first book of the Bible (in English translations). It is a book about beginnings: of the world, of humankind, of civilization, of a people. It sets the stage for an account of how the whole universe is related to the story of a particular people and how the God of that people is in fact the God of the entire world.

The title "Genesis" comes from the earliest Greek translation of the Old Testament (called the Septuagint and widely used by early Christians, who were mostly Greek speakers) and refers to the "genealogy" or "origins" of things as they are. In the Hebrew original (and in contemporary Jewish Bibles), however, the title of the book, in the custom of antiquity, is derived from the first word, *Bereshith,* which translates "In the beginning" or "When."

Genesis as a whole brings together numerous traditions from a variety of sources. One major group of stories is marked by the use of a general term for

God, "Elohim," which will be discussed in due time. These traditions do not comprise a complete narrative. The other set of stories, which uses the personal name YHWH (to be discussed later) in reference to God, presents a fuller narrative, but it, too, is incomplete by itself. These two groups of material are also found in the books of Exodus and Numbers.

The narrative of Genesis, as we have it now, seems to have first been fashioned from its various sources sometime during the reigns of David and Solomon or shortly thereafter, in the middle tenth or middle ninth centuries (950–850 BCE), expressing in part an ideological support for their monarchy. It was edited again later, with additions being made sometime around 530 BCE, after the destruction of Judah in 587 BCE. The purpose of the second and final version was to reflect on what it meant to continue as the people of God in light of the disaster that had befallen Jerusalem, bringing destruction to the Temple and the end of the Davidic monarchy. It is out of this background that we have received the book of Genesis.

The first eleven chapters of Genesis represent an "introduction" to the book (and the Bible) as a whole. They serve to emphasize that the story that is beginning in Genesis is one that is intended to be heard as concerning the whole human family and the entire created order. It is not, as is often mistakenly assumed, a story simply about the prehistory of an ancient people called Israel. Certainly Israel's story does find its beginnings here, but so do the stories of all people, for all are creatures of God in a world fashioned by God.

The "beginnings" of the Bible are highlighted by two primary and inter-related concerns that pertain to all living things. First, there are two accounts of the creation of the world and of humankind preserved as chapters 1–2. Second, there is a long and detailed story about a great flood that marks God's renewed effort at fashioning a world appropriate for creatures intended to live in covenant with God. There are other items of interest to be mentioned along the way, but these two, the initial creation and the new beginning made possible after the great flood, will provide the main focus for this chapter.

## Creation: The Earliest Account

Though it is not the first to appear in Genesis, the earliest account of God's creative work (in terms of when it was written) is preserved in 2:4b–25. The account begins with this simple assertion: "In the day that the LORD God made the earth and the heavens . . ." (2:4b). Three points are immediately established: (1) everything—all that is included in the earth and the heavens—is the result of the divine action; (2) everything is "made," nothing exists in its own right; and (3) the "LORD God" is responsible for all.

The term "LORD God" combines two words used in reference to God throughout the Old Testament. The term "God" renders the Hebrew word *elohim,* a general term quite like our English word "deity." The second term, however, which the New Revised Standard Version renders "LORD," is not a general term at all. It is a proper name, YHWH, revealed to Moses on Mount Sinai (see Exod. 3:13–15). In the course of time, out of respect, the name ceased to be pronounced. Another Hebrew word meaning "Lord" was spoken in its place. Modern scholars suggest "Yahweh" as the proper form of the name, but no one knows for certain. The power of this simple opening declaration is the claim that the One who was later to be known as the Deliverer of Israel from Egypt, the One who would be confessed as God and Father of the Lord Jesus Christ, was the Creator of all that is.

The principal concern of this account is a description of the LORD God's fashioning of a "dirt creature" from the "dirt." With a play on a Hebrew word that means "dirt," "dust," "ground," God is said to have sculptured (rather like a potter) an *adam* (dirt creature) from *adamah* (dirt) (2:7a). To enliven the "earth-ling," God breathed the breath of life into the *adam* (2:7b). So far as the Hebrew text is concerned, the term *adam* was not used as a proper name for the dirt creature until Genesis 5:1. (This in contrast to the Septuagint, which introduced "Adam" as the proper name of the dirt creature in 2:15.) The importance of this tradition is great. Humankind, according to the Hebrew text, was "dirt of dirt, dust of dust," given life and sustained by the one Creator.

As the story unfolds, God with great insight and compassion recognized that the *adam* needed a companion, a helper, a partner. "So out of the ground the LORD God formed every animal of the field and every bird of the air" in order that the dirt creature would not be alone (2:18–19), but "there was not found a helper as his partner" (2:20). Finally, from the bone and flesh of the *adam* the LORD God made a companion and helper appropriate for him who exclaimed, with another play on words:

> "This at last is bone of my bones
>   and flesh of my flesh;
> this one shall be called Woman [*ishshah*],
>   for out of Man [*ish*] this one was taken." (2:23)

With a comment about the significance of marriage (2:24), the story of the creation of all things concludes with the man and woman happy and well, living in a garden planted by God (2:8, 25).

## Creation: The Later Account

The first chapter of Genesis preserves a second, highly structured account of God's creative work. Though it now stands first, it actually was written several centuries later than the story of the dirt creature. This is a reminder that the Bible was not written by one person at one time. Rather, it reflects many different sources produced at many different times. The final book, as we have it, is the result of the work of a company of people who arranged and preserved the materials that they had received for the benefit of subsequent generations.

Genesis 1:1–2:4a is carefully structured. The creative work of God is described as taking place over a six-day period, the activities of days one through three being paralleled by what takes place on days four through six. On day one, for instance, God uttered a word and "light" appeared in the midst of the "formless void and darkness" in which God began (1:2–3). God then proceeded to differentiate the light into day and night (1:4–5). On day four, the day parallel to day one in this liturgy-like prose poem, God is reported to have created the stars, the moon, and the sun (1:14–18). To modern minds this seems strange. If there were day and night at the end of day one, how could the sun and moon not appear until day four? But for the writer of Genesis 1 the point was to show how the universe was structured on days one to three—how the house was built, so to speak—and then how it was filled out on days four to six—or, so to speak, how it was furnished. And at each point along the way, God expressed approval at what had been accomplished: it all was good, "indeed, it was very good" (1:31).

It is worth noting that God's creative work is described in two special ways. First, the primary agent of creation is the divine word. God speaks and something happens (1:3, 6, 9, 11, 14, 20, 24, 26, 28, 29). God doesn't create the world from the split carcass of a defeated rival as in a Babylonian creation story called *Enuma Elish*. No, God simply says, "Let there be. . . ." Much later, in New Testament times, the writer of the Gospel of John will begin his Gospel with these words: "In the beginning was the Word, and the Word was with God, and the Word was God" (John 1:1).

Second, a special Hebrew word, *bara* (create), is used to speak of God's acts of creation. This Hebrew word in the Old Testament (used almost exclusively in Genesis and in the second half of Isaiah) always has God as its subject. In this opening chapter of Genesis it is used in three places. First, in 1:1 we are told, "In the beginning when God created [*bara*] the heavens and the earth. . . ." In other words, the whole foundation of the world as we experience it was wholly the creation of God. Second, God instructs the earth to bring forth "vegetation" (1:11) and "living creatures" (1:24); thus God alone has the power to create (*bara*) the "great sea monsters," which were considered deities in ancient Canaanite and Babylonian mythology, and all the living creatures that come from the waters (1:21). And third, as the climax of God's creative work, God created (*bara*) humankind (1:27; see also 5:1–2; 6:7). In verse 27 the term is repeated three times, dramatically underscoring the importance of the announcement.

On the third day, at divine instruction, the earth brought forth all manner of vegetation (1:11–12). On the sixth day, the parallel day, God created humankind. God said, "'Let us make humankind in our image, according to our likeness . . .'" (1:26). The term translated "humankind" is *adam,* which we have seen in the earlier account first designated humanity rather than a particular individual. Here the collective or generic character of the term is made clear by the plural pronoun that follows: "'let them have dominion. . . .'" According to divine intention humankind was to exercise guardianship over the other living creatures God had created. "Dominion" not "exploitation" was the task (1:26; see also 1:28–30).

Two aspects of the human creature are emphasized. First, God created humankind in God's own image (1:26–27). The term for "image" in Hebrew is *tselem,* which refers usually to a physical likeness or picture of a deity or of a king. Rulers often placed an image or a statue of themselves at the borders of their land to make clear whose country one was entering. The images of the deities worshiped by a conquering king or general were at times placed in the sanctuaries of the defeated to remind them of whose god was the more powerful. Here in Genesis God creates humans in the image of God. Humans are God's representatives in the world; they remind the world and one another of the identity of the creator and of the responsibility God has given to humankind.

The second important aspect of God's creation is that from the outset of their creation humans were differentiated as males and females (1:27). While some might interpret the earlier creation story to suggest that "woman" was somehow subordinate to "man," such an understanding is not supported by this later account. God created male and female together in the divine image and blessed them for their work in God's world (1:27–28). The implications of this radical assertion are still being worked out in the community of faith, but its startling vision has been instructive for all who cared to consider it for over two millennia.

A consideration of this later account of God's creative work would be incomplete without the recognition of where this whole, beautifully structured prose poem led for the earliest readers/hearers. The creation of the heavens and the earth and all that was in them was completed in six days. And then there was a seventh day, a day of divine rest (2:3). Genesis is not a scientific treatise, however, and the term "day" need not be taken in an absolutely literal manner. Nonetheless, an important point is being made. Not only the space but also the time of the universe belong to God. Here in the very beginning, as a culmination of the creation of the heavens and the earth, the Creator God rested on day seven and hallowed it for all time (2:2–3). Later, in the book of Exodus, God's "rest" or "sabbath" will be cited as the basis for the mandate that all living things should observe a day of rest, a Sabbath, once every seven days (Exod. 20:8–11; 31:12–17).

## The Flood and Its Prelude

If the story had stopped at the end of Genesis 2, the human situation would have been good. Created in God's image, male and female (Gen. 1), and placed in a beautiful garden in a happy innocence (Gen. 2), what more could humankind need?

But unfortunately, the story did not end there. Genesis 3 reports a breakdown of relationship between the humans and God and God's subsequent expulsion of Adam and Eve from the garden of Eden (3:24). Following immediately is a story of enmity between the children of Adam and Eve that culminates with Cain's murder of his brother Abel (4:1–16).

Chapter 5 preserves a genealogy of "Adam's" descendants. This is the first time the term *adam* (as noted above) is used as a proper name in the Hebrew text (5:1). It is reported that Adam had other children not mentioned in the story or genealogy (5:4). The genealogy is introduced with a reference to 1:27–28 and God's creation of humankind in the divine image. The genealogy is preceded with references to the emergence of seminomadic life (4:20), the appearance of the lyre and the pipe (4:21), and the development of bronze and iron tools (4:22). The interesting note is preserved (contrary to the claim of Exod. 3:13–15 as previously noted) that during the time when Enosh was born "people began to invoke the name of the LORD" (4:26). This is another indication of the folklore traditions that have been preserved.

The downward slide of the human family culminates in great wickedness. In a very strange account, "sons of God" (the term usually refers to divine beings of some sort) are said to have intermarried with mortal women (6:2). The origins of this tradition are unknown, but it is linked with another ancient story about giants, the Nephilim, who at one time roamed the earth (6:4). It is impossible to "verify" this story, but for the editors of Genesis it provided the transition to a most important assertion: "The LORD saw that the wickedness of humankind was great in the earth, and that every inclination of the thoughts of their hearts was only evil continually. And the LORD was sorry that he had made humankind on the earth, and it grieved him to his heart" (6:5–6). Thus the LORD decided, "'I will blot out from the earth the human beings I have created . . . for I am sorry that I have made them'" (6:7).

Two very important points are made here. First, the great flood that is the main subject of the middle chapters of Genesis (6–9) was not a capricious act by an immoral deity. Great care is taken to describe the "wickedness" that had become rampant among humans. Unlike the stories about the deities that were told by others in the ancient Near East—stories of jealous, vengeful, demanding gods and goddesses—this story is about a Creator who is deeply saddened by the evil that humankind exhibits. Rather than a tale of inescapable "fate" so loved by the Greeks, it was a story of moral failure on the part of the humans that God had created. Humans had brought violence and corruption to the earth (6:5, 11–12). God's judgment was more than justified.

Second, this story makes clear that the divine Creator has "feelings" and can change direction. Human wickedness "grieved" God and brought pain to God's heart (6:6). God is described in terms of sorrow rather than anger (6:7). Human behavior matters to God! The biblical story unfolds in a demonstration of how God continually adjusted to the increasing disappointment brought by humankind's willful disregard of God's intentions. Judgment and forgiveness are both aspects of divine care for the world, and both are as deeply connected to humankind as to God (see also Exod. 34:6–7; Ps. 103:8; Jonah 4:2).

In fact, it is the mercy of God that precludes a total end of the human story. Though God was deeply saddened at what humans had done, and though God decided to "blot out from the earth the human beings" God had created (6:7, 13), God nonetheless chose to provide a continuation of humankind through one person named Noah on whom God looked graciously (6:8). That Noah can be described as a "righteous man, blameless in his generation" (6:9) is a result of the favor he found in God's sight, not the reason for divine mercy. Having been chosen by God, Noah carried out his assignment faithfully and therein showed himself to be "righteous." In the Bible "righteousness" is not primarily a moral category so much as a relational one. If one faithfully fulfills the expectations of one's role, then one is righteous, and this is what Noah did (see Gen. 38:24–26).

## The Flood and Its Aftermath

The story of the flood is at the center of the introduction to the Bible preserved in Genesis 1–11. From 6:11 through 8:19 the details of the flood and the escape from it by Noah, his family, and the animals and birds brought into the ark (7:13–14) are recounted. It appears that two slightly different versions of the story have been woven together. On the one hand, in 6:19–21 we are told that a pair of each type of animal and bird was to be preserved while, on the other hand, in 7:2–4 Noah was instructed to take seven pairs of all clean animals onboard along with one pair of unclean animals. There are other such duplications and discrepancies, but to become too caught up in them is to miss the point.

Likewise, it is an unnecessary distraction to get drawn into a literalizing of the story on the basis that there are flood stories preserved by numerous peoples around the world. While that is true, two disclaimers should be made. First, there is no credible archaeological or geological evidence for one worldwide flood. The various flood stories that have been preserved are dated to widely different times, sometimes hundreds of years apart. Second, there are many places, Palestine for instance, that do not have a local flood story at all. To get caught up in questions of the historicity of the account in Genesis is to risk missing the point.

So what is the point? What is the reader intended to recognize and acknowledge? There are at least three key points. First, though God decided to destroy the world because of the corruption that had filled it (6:11–13), nonetheless God did not give up on the human project. Rather, God chose one man, Noah, and his family to be delivered from the flood in order to preserve humankind (6:18–19; 7:1). Second, at the conclusion of the flood God acknowledges a sacrifice made by Noah and promises, "'I will never again curse the ground because of humankind, for the inclination of the human heart is evil from youth; nor will I ever again destroy every living creature as I have done'" (8:21). Humankind, and indeed all living creatures, would from thenceforth be able to count on the regular rotation of the seasons without threat of divinely delivered destruction (8:22). In the third place, God established a covenant with all flesh (9:9–11) and placed the rainbow (the Hebrew term can also refer to a war bow) in the heavens as an everlasting reminder of the grace under which humans and all flesh would live forever (9:12–17). This covenant was not based on human obedience; it was totally dependent on divine grace! God can be trusted!

## Conclusion

At the end of the flood story, God makes clear that to accomplish the divine agenda will require a different approach. Humans will continue to be headstrong and set on their own aims (see the story of Babel in Gen. 11:1–9). God, on the other hand, will begin anew, starting with one particular family despite the clear imperfection of its members (Gen. 9:20–27), to establish the community God desires. The story of the "beginnings" sketches in bold relief the intentions of a loving Creator toward the whole human family.

While the narrative in Genesis will become more narrowly focused on the forebears of Israel, the introduction presented in chapters 1–11 continues to remind us that this is a story about us all, a story intended for us all. Much more than history, it is theology, a theology that points us toward a loving, merciful Creator who longs for an ongoing relationship with all humanity.

# *Chapter Two*
# A Promise Is a Promise

## *A Study of Genesis 12:1–20; 17:1–27; 22:1–19*

Chapters 12–50 of Genesis preserve stories about the predecessors of the people of Israel. The stories begin with a divine promise received by Abram and Sarai (they don't receive the names Abraham and Sarah until 17:5, 15) and then reveal the unfolding of that promise across several generations. Attention to the promise provides the dramatic structure for Genesis as a whole, and particularly for the stories about Abraham and Sarah (12–24) that will be the main focus of this chapter. The point of the narrative is that the promise is powerful and reliable because the promise giver, God, is absolutely trustworthy.

The story begins in Ur, which, to the best of our knowledge, was located in what is now Iraq, about two hundred miles southeast of Baghdad and one hundred miles northwest of the border with Kuwait, on the banks of the Euphrates River. There Abram and his wife Sarai lived with Abram's father, Terah, and others of the extended family (Gen. 11:27–32). They were Urites, Mesopotamians, not Israelites. At this point in the account God selects a particular Mesopotamian family—as was the case with Noah—to continue the project of fashioning a human community fitting in God's sight.

For reasons not entirely clear, the whole clan left to go to Canaan, about one

---

thousand miles away from Ur at the opposite end of the Fertile Crescent. The Fertile Crescent is an arch of land that extends from the mouth of the Tigris and Euphrates Rivers up to what is now Turkey, and then down along the Mediterranean Sea through parts of modern Syria, Lebanon, and Israel/Palestine to Egypt. They probably moved along established trade routes. But they did not make it to Canaan. Instead they stopped in Haran, a city located in what is now southeast Turkey.

## The Initial Promise

It was in Haran that somewhat out of the blue, so to speak, the LORD spoke to Terah's son Abram. Was this a literal encounter like we might have with someone at a coffee shop, or is this a literary device chosen as a way to unfold the narrative? There is no way to be certain, but probably the latter. In light of what we have already discovered in the Noah story, it is best not to read Genesis as a literal, empirically factual account. It is a theological narrative, and the point is clear: God at God's own initiative and choosing established a relationship with Abram and Sarai based on a promise.

Abram and Sarai were instructed to leave Haran to go to a land initially unidentified (12:1). YHWH intended to make of them a "great nation," making them "a great name" (famous) and "a blessing" (12:2). Through Abram and Sarai all the peoples of the world were to receive a blessing (12:3). Later in the story this promise is repeated and sealed with a covenant (17:1–22; see also 15:7–21), the sign of which was the rite of circumcision (17:10). Abram became Abraham, and Sarai, Sarah (17:5, 15). Because of this promise to Abraham and his response to it, Abram the Urite was remembered in the Bible as Abraham, "the friend of God" (Isa. 41:8; 2 Chr. 20:7; Jas. 2:23).

Abram and Sarai, along with a nephew, Lot, left Haran and traveled with their households and flocks south to the land of Canaan (12:4–5). They stopped at Shechem (located near present-day Nablus) in the heart of Canaan's hill country. In the course of time they proceeded several hundred miles farther south to the Negev, a great semiarid area with terrain rather like that found in southern New Mexico and Arizona (12:6–9). Eventually they even reached Egypt (12:10). While in Shechem, Abram received the additional word that God intended to give "this land" to Abram's offspring, literally his "seed" (12:7). It is important to note, however, that the exact boundaries of "this land" are not specified.

## Testing the Promise

While Abram and Sarai are remembered for their trusting response to the divine promise, Abram's first action does not seem so faithful. Immediately after the account of the events at Shechem the narrative presents Abram and Sarai going to Egypt to escape a drought-caused famine in Canaan (12:10). Before they entered the land, Abram, afraid that the Egyptians would kill him in order to take Sarai because of her great beauty, instructed Sarai to tell them she was his sister (12:11–13). Rather than trust that God would protect this couple to whom a divine promise of offspring had been given, Abram decided to rely on human trickery.

The Egyptian officials were indeed dazzled by Sarai's beauty. They went to Pharaoh and told him about the entry of this beautiful woman into the land, and Pharaoh, having been told that Sarai was Abram's unmarried sister, had her brought into his harem. Because of Sarai, Abram received great wealth in the form of livestock and a multitude of servants from the hand of Pharaoh. From the point of view of the narrative, however, the promise was jeopardized. Sarai, who was to bear the child of the divine promise, was radically compromised (12:14–16). How could she be the mother of Abram's promised heir if she became one of Pharaoh's many wives?

In this episode, God intervened by afflicting Pharaoh and his household with plagues (12:17; see 20:18). Pharaoh recognized that Abram had falsely introduced Sarai as his sister rather than his wife (12:18–19). Acknowledging his wrongdoing in taking the wife of another into his harem, Pharaoh released Sarai and sent Abram on his way (12:20; see 20:17–18). In misleading Pharaoh as he did, Abram showed little trust in God.

The narrator has used the divine promise of progeny and land as a motif to illustrate a lack of confidence in God on the part of the main characters in this story in Genesis. The lack of trust in God's promise is encountered in several different ways in the stories about Abram and Sarai. Repeatedly, rather than trust God to deliver on the promise of a child, for instance, Abram and Sarai take matters into their own hands. On the one hand, they each set out on their own to provide an heir for Abram. Abram chose Eliezer, a slave born in his house (possibly sired by Abram), as his designated heir (15:1–3). Sarai gave her maidservant Hagar to Abram and told him to have intercourse with her so that she might conceive and bear an heir for Abram (16:1–4). Later, in the city of Gerar ruled by Abimelech, Abraham chose to ensure his own safety while putting Sarah at great risk (20:1–18). Abraham apparently didn't trust God to protect Sarah, the one who was to mother the heir that God had promised. In these stories neither Abraham nor Sarah are presented as the paragons of faith that later generations have made of them.

It is important to listen to these stories in all their particularity and unevenness. Abraham and Sarah were not selected because they were especially virtuous or brave or faithful. They were average people with good traits and bad. Sometimes they responded in the ways God hoped; at other times they did not. The point is that God determined to set out directing humankind toward God's goal and drawing us all into God's way by working with and through very ordinary people with whom just about anyone can identify.

## Living in Covenant

As previously mentioned, the promise of God given to Abraham and Sarah was understood in terms of a covenant, a *berith*. There are two main forms of covenant in the Bible, and each is instituted solely at the initiative of God. One is patterned after what is called a suzerainty treaty, used in the ancient Middle East by one king (the suzerain) with lesser kings (his vassals). This kind of treaty has stipulations that must be kept by the vassal in return for the protection of the suzerain. The covenant God made with Moses at Mount Sinai was of this type, a conditional covenant, one that had stipulations (commandments) that were to be followed by the human partners in order to maintain the arrangement (see Exod. 20–23).

The covenant that God made with Abraham and Sarah described in 17:1–14, however, was of a quite different type. It was a promissory covenant dependent solely on the trustworthiness of the one who made the promise. This kind of covenant was patterned after promissory grants made in the ancient Middle East, usually involving the gift of land by a king or a member of nobility to someone without land. This promise was given solely on the basis of divine initiative. The covenant God made with Noah was also a promissory covenant. Abram did not "earn" God's favor any more than had Noah. For reasons known only to God, Abram and Sarai were singled out as the people through whom God would continue God's project with humankind. God freely established and guaranteed the relationship. Humans may learn faithfulness in the process of living in such a covenant, but their response is not the foundation on which the relationship depends.

The circumstances of the actual covenant-making ceremony are described once (15:7–11, 17–21) in terms of a sacrifice and a second time in terms of an accompanying rite. In the first instance Abraham is directed to bring several animals and birds, cut them in half, and arrange the halves over against one another (15:7–11). Then, when the sun had set, God, represented by a "smoking fire pot and a flaming torch," passed between the remains of the animals and birds. This act was understood to seal the promise. In effect it meant that God agreed to be slaughtered in the same fashion as the animals and birds if the divine promise was not kept (15:17). God took the sole responsibility and risk to keep the covenant while not requiring anything of Abraham or Sarah. The content of the covenant was the divine promise: to the descendants of Abraham was given the land "from the river of Egypt to the great river, the river Euphrates" (15:18–21).

This promise of land has been understood in a number of different ways across the centuries. In contemporary times it is put forward by some Jews who see themselves as the descendants of Abraham as warrant for the occupation of the whole area known as Palestine. But Christians and Muslims also believe that they are the descendants of Abraham and thus dispute the right of Jews to claim the promise alone. Further, some point to the destruction of Judah in the sixth century as an indication that Israel lost the land because of disobedience to God's way.

The boundaries of the land in question have also been variously marked in the Bible. There is not one single definition that all would acknowledge. At the height of the Davidic-Solomonic United Kingdom in the tenth century BCE, the land under control by Israel extended from the port of Elath on the Gulf of Elath/Aqaba to well above the Sea of Galilee, and from the Mediterranean Sea to parts of the land on the east side of the Jordan. Is that the land of promise? In most places much more modest claims are made. This is mentioned here to underscore how carefully one must interpret the Bible lest it be misused in a literalistic manner or dismissed as only some kind of a fairy tale.

In the second passage where the promise is linked to covenant language, a specific rite is designated as the sign of the covenant that God made with Abraham and Sarah, namely, the rite of circumcision (17:9–14). The removal of the foreskins of all the males of the community became the sign of acceptance of the covenant. It was not done to establish the relationship—that was done strictly on divine initiative. But in response to God's promise and as an external sign of the covenant, God instructed that all males were to be circumcised. This rite is still practiced by Jews to this day.

In the ancient Middle East circumcision was not unique to those who later came to be called Israelites. So far as we know, all the western Semites practiced circumcision. The practice became important as a distinguishing mark at two times in Israel's history, however, when there was close contact with two hostile groups: (1) the Philistines, who as non-Semites were uncircumcised; and (2) the Babylonians, who as eastern Semites did not practice circumcision. It should be noted that Abraham was remembered as an eastern Semite, a Urite, who traveled to the west and thereby became a western Semite. The story in Genesis as we now have it was probably crafted and placed in the narrative during or after the sixth century BCE, after many Judeans had suffered exile in Babylon. This sign of the covenant became especially important to them at that time. In the subsequent history of Judaism, circumcision has continued as a sign of belonging to a group of people that believes it is in a special relationship with God.

There is another dimension to God's covenant with Abraham and Sarah, however. After the promise had been reiterated by God (17:4), and Abram's name had been changed to Abraham (17:5: the Hebrew was interpreted to mean "father" or "ancestor" of "multitudes"), Abraham questioned how this might be, for Sarah was already ninety years old (17:17). So, he prayed that God would bless Ishmael as his heir, a son who had been born to Abraham by Sarah's slave (17:18). God responded by assuring Abraham that Sarah would indeed bear Abraham an heir, Isaac (17:19), but that God would also bless Ishmael and "make him a great nation" (17:20). Ishmael has come to be understood as the forebear of those Arabs who centuries later became Muslims.

## Passing the Quality Test

The climax of the Abraham/Sarah narrative comes in chapter 22. The story begins abruptly with "After these things God tested Abraham" (22:1). In the King James translation "tempt" is chosen to render the Hebrew word where the New Revised Standard Version has better used "test." In either instance, common use of either term may mislead the average reader. The Hebrew word, *nissah*, as used in this context, does not mean to "quiz" or to "trick," and certainly does not mean to pose a "temptation." Here *nissah*, to test/tempt, is used in the sense of "testing one's mettle," of examining the readiness of someone for a task, of enabling one to demonstrate one's reliability.

The story begins by announcing that this is what God is doing with respect to Abraham, "testing his readiness." In the same manner, God will later determine the readiness of the people of Israel to trust God (see Exod. 16:4; 20:20; Deut. 8:2). The psalmist was using the term in a similar manner when praying,

> Prove me, O LORD, and try me;
> test my heart and mind.
> *(Ps. 26:2)*

In other words, prays the psalmist, "See if I am ready." The writer of the New Testament book of Hebrews rightly understood the nuance of the Genesis text and acknowledged Abraham's trust in God (Heb. 11:17). Thus, from the very outset of this account we know that God is up to something good, not something bad.

The account is known to Christians as "the sacrifice of Isaac" and has been a theme in religious art for centuries. In Jewish tradition the story is known as "the binding of Isaac" because that is in fact much more accurate. The narrator does tell us that Abraham bound Isaac and readied him for sacrifice (22:9–10), but—and this is one of the main points of the story—Isaac was not sacrificed (22:12)!

To jump too quickly to the end of the story, though, is to miss the drama. Remember that this is the climactic episode in a narrative where Abraham has repeatedly demonstrated his incapacity to trust fully in God. Once again God addresses Abraham and now instructs him to take his only son to a distant place to offer his son as a burnt offering (22:2). Abraham's deep relationship with Isaac is underscored; Isaac is "your [Abraham's] son, your only son Isaac, whom you love" (22:2)! The offering was to be a total one, a burnt offering. The reader—and this story is for adults, not children!—can only wonder at this point as to what was going on in Abraham's mind, or in Isaac's or Sarah's for that matter. How do you tolerate hearing such an instruction or even consider carrying it out? What was God thinking about?

Knowing the outcome as we do—and remember, God, the loving God, the God who promised Abraham and Sarah an heir, that God is the one in charge of this story—we can appreciate the dramatic manner in which the account is developed. We are told that Abraham and Isaac, with two other young men, cut wood for the sacrifice (22:3) and then traveled for three days toward the land of Moriah, which was in later tradition identified with Jerusalem (see 2 Chr. 3:1).

After instructing the young men with him to stay at a certain place and wait for his return, Abraham set out with Isaac for the appointed place. He carried the knife and fire for the sacrifice, while Isaac carried the wood (22:6). How long did they walk? What was going on between them? The only recorded dialogue between father and son was prompted by Isaac's observation and question "'The fire and the wood are here, but where is the lamb for a burnt offering?'" (22:7). Was Isaac beginning to deduce what was about to happen? Abraham responded ambiguously: "'God himself will provide the lamb for a burnt offering, my son'" (22:8).

When they arrived at the "place that God had shown him"—we are not told how this happened—Abraham built an altar, laid the wood on it, and then bound Isaac and placed him on top of the wood (22:9). While Abraham is remembered for his trust, Isaac shows quite a bit as well. He was old enough to carry the wood for the altar; he was the child of the promise; but he trusted himself to his father. Why didn't he run or resist in some fashion or at least protest? We are not given any answers to our questions. But at the last possible moment, as the tension in the story becomes almost unbearable, God through a divine messenger or angel intervened and stopped the impending sacrifice. Abraham's trusting obedience was recognized by God (22:11–12). Abraham was pointed to a ram that was caught in a nearby thicket. The ram was offered as the burnt offering. Abraham's beloved son was spared (22:13).

One of the outcomes of this story in ancient Israel was that child sacrifice was forever banned as an inappropriate way to show reverence to God. The people were to "fear" God or, in other words, to reverence God and stand in "awe" before the divine (22:12). Unlike the practice among some of the neighboring peoples, however, in Israel human sacrifice, though sometimes conducted, was not condoned from the time of Abraham on (see Judg. 11:34–40; 2 Kgs. 16:3; Ezek. 20:26, 31).

The more immediate and obvious outcome in terms of the Abraham/Sarah narrative was the reaffirmation of the divine promise. As the story had begun, now in light of Abraham's demonstration of his trust in God, the LORD once again promised offspring to Abraham and Sarah "as numerous as the stars of heaven and as the sand that is on the seashore" (22:17). Because Abraham obeyed God's voice, his offspring was to be the source of blessing for all the nations of the earth (22:18).

Having reached its zenith, the story is brought to a conclusion with some genealogical notes (22:20–24) and the account of Sarah's death and burial "at Kiriath-arba (that is, Hebron) in the land of Canaan" (23:2, 19–20). This final note is important in that it makes clear that Abraham and Sarah did in fact acquire a place in the land promised to their offspring. Though it was only a small piece, a cave to the east of Mamre purchased from a Hittite named Ephron, son of Zohar (23:6–16), it represented a "partial fulfillment" of the divine promise. The text makes it clear that Abraham bought the "field with the cave that was in it and all the trees that were in the field" (23:17). While a small thing, the mention of the "trees" serves to help locate the tradition historically since "trees" were especially important to note in Hittite land sales in the second millennium BCE. At his death Abraham was also buried in this cave (25:7–10). The traditional site of their burial is still venerated by Jews and Muslims in the contemporary city of Hebron.

## Conclusion

The narrative about Abram/Abraham and Sarai/Sarah begins and ends with a divine promise, a promise that is tantamount to a covenant. The story unfolds with the giving of the promise, with threats to the realization of the promise, and with the concrete though partial keeping of the promise. Both faithfulness and faithlessness are noted. The characters are "three dimensional" in that their faults and virtues are both articulated.

Throughout the narrative the clear aim is to highlight God's ongoing perseverance and commitment. We can trust in the divine covenant with the forebears of humankind because God, the promise giver, is totally trustworthy. There are many interesting tidbits of information found in the materials we have briefly surveyed—names of long-forgotten places and people, hints of traditions and practices long lost—but the most important point in the whole account is that God began a story with Abraham and Sarah and, true to the divine promise, will bring it to an appropriate conclusion.

*Chapter Three*

# Human Choice
# and Divine Purpose

*A Study of Genesis 24:1–67*

## Introduction

Good stories have structure and development. They start and end and have marks all along the way to keep the reader/listener attentive and engaged. Genesis is such a narrative, beginning with the creation of the world (Gen. 1) and concluding with the preservation of a particular people (Gen. 50). All along the way are key accounts that move the narrative forward while highlighting various important elements of the composition. The story about the marriage of Rebekah and Isaac is one such episode in the Genesis drama.

This story is placed almost at the center of the book of Genesis and is the longest single episode (sixty-seven verses) in the account. It marks a critical moment in the story: the emergence of the next generation, the next human link necessary for the continuation of the divine plan put in motion by God's giving a promise of progeny and land to Abraham and Sarah. It is well told and deserves close attention for both its literary character and its theological implications. Humans are clearly at the center of the story, but a divine plan is being implemented. Without human participation God's purpose cannot be met. Without divine intention human activity is finally meaningless.

## The Narrative Setting

The account begins when "Abraham was old, well advanced in years" (24:1). At its conclusion, Abraham's death at the good old age of one hundred seventy-five is noted (25:7–8). While the specific numbers may be questioned—there is no evidence that people of antiquity lived the long lives often attributed to them— the point is clear: Abraham died of natural causes after a long and fruitful life (25:1–6).

Abraham and his family were living in Hebron in the land of Canaan (23:19–20; 25:9–10). Hebron is located about twenty miles south-southwest of Jerusalem. At an elevation of 3,040 feet above sea level, Hebron is the highest populated center in the southern hill country, even higher than Jerusalem, which is situated at around 2,300 to 2,500 feet above sea level. As noted in chapter 2, Hebron served as the burial site for both Abraham and Sarah. Today, there is a shrine at the site that is especially holy for Jews and Muslims; it bears the Arabic name Haram el-Khalil ("the sacred area of the friend," "friend" being a reference to Abraham known in tradition as the "friend" of God).

The "problem" that had to be addressed at this point in the Genesis drama concerned the assurance that Isaac would have a proper wife to bear the child who could carry forward the promise of God. A marriage was going to have to be arranged, but since they were living among Canaanites, not just any available young woman would do (24:3). Someone had to travel back to the region of Haran, Abraham's home, to find an appropriate wife for Isaac from among Abraham's kin (24:4). Modern Westerners may find arranged marriages rather strange, but they were the norm in ancient communities and still are in many parts of the world. Marriage was an economic as well as a societal institution, and larger family interests had to be met. Though a Semite, Abraham was not a Canaanite, and connections with his wider clan, Abraham's "kindred" (24:4) and his "father's house" (24:7), though geographically distant, were important and had to be honored. "Romantic love" (contrary to contemporary Western understanding) usually had little place in the process. Isaac needed a wife, and Abraham selected a trusted servant to carry out the necessary negotiations to procure Isaac a partner (24:2).

This issue drives the narrative. The narrator will develop the story and allow us to follow along, engaging as we will. It is a story with action, suspense, and surprise. We need to read it expectantly yet with patience. As it slowly but steadily unfolds, the skill and sensitivity of the narrator will become clear. It is a story well told that deserves our close attention.

## But What If?

Human life is marked by multiple "what ifs." What if this happens; what if that happens? Will the picnic go on if it rains? Will the marriage take place if the bride's mother gets sick? What if the market turns bad? What if? Many things simply cannot be controlled; there are too many possible contingencies. Is it ever wise to make set plans? This tension is built into this narrative from the outset.

To set the search for a wife for Isaac in motion, Abraham asked his oldest, most trusted "servant" (the word literally means "slave") to take an oath (24:2). (Perhaps this slave was the Eliezer mentioned in 15:2.) The mode of the oath taking is unclear, though the servant was instructed to place his hand "'under [Abraham's] thigh'" as he swore by "'the LORD, the God of heaven and earth'" to carry out Abraham's wishes (24:2–3, 9). The Hebrew term translated "thigh" can refer to the upper fleshy part of the leg ("from the hips to the thighs," Exod. 28:42), or it can refer to a male's genitals, the source of his procreative powers (Gen. 32:32; 46:26; 47:29). Exactly how the term is used in the context of oath taking is debated, but it seems to indicate that the one taking the oath placed a hand in a very intimate place as a sign of earnestness and trustworthiness.

The instructions that the servant swore to carry out were to travel northward to Haran to find a bride for Isaac. Under no circumstances was a Canaanite woman to be selected (24:3–4), as she would not be part of Abraham's kindred, his clan. As the term "Canaanite" is used in this passage, it apparently was understood to include all the peoples that inhabited the land into which Abraham had traveled, including the "Hittites" from whom Abraham had purchased his plot in Hebron (23:19; see 15:19–21).

The servant, the oldest and most trusted servant of Abraham's household, had been, you might say, around the block more than once (24:2). He knew how difficult humans could be, how uncooperative, how shortsighted. The servant was quite aware that his was going to be a difficult task. One doesn't just waltz in out of nowhere and convince a young woman to leave her family to travel to a distant land to become the bride of someone she's never heard of in a place she's never been. What if, just what if, she refused?

The servant posed such a possibility to Abraham. If he could not persuade anyone to return with him, should he then take Isaac to Haran (24:5)? Abraham was adamantly opposed to such an alternative! Under no circumstance was Isaac to be taken back to Haran (24:6). God's promise required that Isaac continue to live in the land of Canaan, where his inheritance lay (24:7). Abraham assured his servant that God would send "his angel" before him to assist in the search (24:7). Exactly what kind of help was envisioned is not clear, but the point is that God had been and would continue to be involved in the process.

Abraham expressed no doubt that the servant's mission would be a success.

Nonetheless, with a nod to human realities and in acknowledgment that human decision, which cannot safely be coerced, is always necessary in the unfolding of life, Abraham offers an "out." If, in fact, the servant after a diligent search could not find a young woman willing to return to Canaan to be Isaac's bride, then the servant would be released from his oath. The servant was still not to take Isaac there, but the servant could return with impunity (24:8). This "what if" is the thematic power that fuels the remainder of the story. "What if" is what we read on to determine.

## Finding Rebekah

The three-hundred-mile journey northward from Hebron to Aram-naharaim, the city of Nahor, Abraham's brother (11:27), is reported in one verse (24:10). Accompanied by a number of men (24:32), the trusted servant had taken ten camels loaded with gifts for the prospective bride's family (24:10). But the trip itself, which was not as safe or easy as travel today, was inconsequential to the story. Thus, one verse!

Much more important to the narrator was the arrival and the prayer that the servant made to God. They had reached Aram-naharaim in the late afternoon. The men and the camels rested outside the city by the well (24:11). The women of the city were coming out, each carrying a large water jar on her shoulders, to draw from the well for the needs of their families for the night (24:13). Apparently Abraham's servant knew he had reached the correct town, but he still had the very real problem of locating the right person. So he prayed that God would help identify the young woman that he was looking for through her words and actions (24:14).

The prayer was directed to the LORD, the God of his master Abraham, asking for success by God's continuation of "steadfast love" (sometimes translated "kindness" or "mercy") to Abraham (24:12). "Steadfast love" is a phrase often used in covenantal formulations that signals a quality of commitment that is unshakeable. Though human decision would be necessary, divine direction was most desired. The servant asked simply enough that the intended woman be identified in two ways: (1) by her willingness to give water to the servant and (2) by her willingness also to water his camels (24:14a). She needed to be hospitable and strong! If she were nice looking, that would be a plus! Were this prayer to be answered positively, the servant would be assured that God's "steadfast love" for Abraham continued (24:14b).

The narrator allows the reader/hearer to know who Rebekah is well before Abraham's servant learns her identity (24:15, 23–24). Rebekah was the granddaughter of Abraham's brother Nahor and his wife Milcah; her father was

Bethuel, a cousin of Isaac (24:15; see 11:29). She also had a brother, Laban, who will figure prominently in the story before it is over (24:28ff). The narrator informs us that Rebekah was old enough and strong enough to be sent out to get water for her family and that she was "fair to look upon, a virgin" (24:15–16). Presumably her status as a "virgin" was signaled by the clothing or jewelry she wore. However that may be, the reader/hearer is immediately alerted to expect a good outcome from this chance encounter.

When Rebekah was coming up from the well, Abraham's servant ran to her and asked for a sip of water. The identifying behavior was about to be made manifest. She immediately gave him a drink and then set about drawing water for the camels as well (24:17–20). Surely this was sufficient indication that this young woman was the one sought for Isaac. Hadn't she done exactly what the servant had asked? But the narrator, ever the skillful storyteller, stretched the drama a little further by commenting that "the man gazed at her in silence to learn whether or not the LORD had made his journey successful" (24:21). The repetitious character of the narrative may seem strange to modern readers/hearers, but it is a technique frequently found in ancient stories. A library of ancient Canaanite literature has been found at Ugarit in Syria, and some of the accounts found there reflect the same repetitive style.

How long the watering of ten camels took we can only imagine, but it certainly was not completed in a brief moment. All the while that Rebekah made repeated trips down to the well and back, Abraham's servant watched and wondered. When she had completed the task, the servant took a "gold nose-ring weighing a half shekel, and two bracelets for her arms weighing ten gold shekels" (24:22). It is impossible to assign a specific value to these gifts in contemporary terms. Values then as now fluctuate. Right now silver per ounce is worth a little more than gold per ounce, but that is not always the case. Whatever the value, the gift was certainly, at least, a very nice "tip."

Then came the moment all the audience had been waiting for. "'Tell me,'" said the servant, "'whose daughter you are'" and, he asked, "'Is there room in your father's house for us to spend the night?'" (24:23). The revelation that Rebekah was of the house of Nahor ("the daughter of Bethuel son of Milcah, whom she bore to Nahor") and that there was plenty of room at their house for the servant and his men to stay (24:24–25) prompted the servant to offer an immediate prayer of thanksgiving "'Blessed be the LORD, the God of my master Abraham,'" for God's "'steadfast love'" and "'faithfulness'" toward Abraham indeed continued (24:27). "Faithfulness" translates a Hebrew term that means "firm" and "trustworthy." These are the divine qualities that upheld the promise of God and provided the basis on which to move forward into the unknown. What's more and most gratifying, the servant had been led right to the house of Abraham's kindred just as he had asked.

## Meeting with the Family

The development of the narrative manifests a style not common in modern Western literature. The story moves forward, to be sure, but with a great deal of reiteration of dialogue and narrative. Rebekah ran to her home and reported what had happened (24:28). Her brother Laban, before (24:29) or after (24:30) he saw the gifts bestowed on his sister, ran to the well-spring to meet Abraham's servant and to welcome him into his house (24:30–31). The narrative seems to skip a transition because the next thing we read is that Laban, the servant, and the whole entourage are at Laban's house and are being invited in (24:31). Whatever the case, the servant's animals were cared for, and water was provided so that the travelers could wash their feet, an important custom of the time (24:32). Note that all of this activity, which would certainly have taken some time to accomplish, is briefly reported in two verses.

The narrator knows what needs to be emphasized and hastens to move on. In a way that would have seemed rude or at least in poor taste, the servant refused to eat food that had been prepared for him until he explained how he came to be there and the purpose of his visit (24:33). The etiquette of hospitality that Laban extended to the servant usually included the sharing of a meal. To put this off until "business" was conducted meant that the hospitality was not yet accepted, at least not to the level of establishing a relationship of reciprocity. The servant was unwilling to become any more "indebted" to Laban before Laban knew of the servant's mission. So he asked to speak and was granted that opportunity.

At this point in the narrative there is a retelling of all that has happened. As already noted, this may seem to many moderns as unnecessarily redundant. Of course, in one sense it is, but from the point of view of the storyteller—and totally in keeping with the craft as practiced in the Middle East several thousand years ago—it was important to heighten the anticipation of the audience. The story of Abraham's acquired wealth (24:35) and the heir born to Sarah in her old age (24:36) was shared. The task assigned to find a wife for the heir from among Abraham's own kindred, the sworn oath, and even the "what if" stipulation were reported (24:37–41). A slight variation is introduced into the story: not only might the woman choose not to return with the servant, but the family might also be reluctant to let her go (24:39, 41; see 24:5, 8). A little more tension is thereby introduced into the account.

The servant next described his encounter with Rebekah at the well. He told of his prayer and how he hoped God would lead him to the right person (24:42–44). He reported how Rebekah had suddenly appeared, shown great hospitality, and had then identified herself as part of Abraham's kindred (24:45–47). The servant acknowledged his prayer of thanksgiving to God for having led him to Rebekah (24:48). But then the servant could only wait to see if their human judgment would confirm or deny his sense of having come to the correct place. Would they, the servant asked, employing the same Hebrew terminology used to describe God's dealing with Abraham (24:12, 27), deal "loyally and truly" with his master Abraham (24:49)?

## Human Decision Matters

Perhaps the storyteller paused for a moment to let the gravity of the situation sink in. Humans often make decisions that ignore, or at least cause detours in accomplishing, God's purpose. Why should Laban (Rebekah's brother) or Bethuel (Rebekah's father) believe the unnamed servant of a long-absent kinsman living in the remote land of Canaan and to them a complete stranger? Why should they send away their sister and daughter to be a bride of the heir of this fellow named Abraham? The narrative reaches a point of high tension.

Somewhat unexpectedly, Laban and Bethuel agree to the servant's request (24:50)! In effect, they say, "How can we dispute your story that this all comes from the LORD?" Apparently they believed the testimony of the servant that God had led him to this place and to Rebekah. Was faith in the God of Abraham so strong among his kindred? The text does not reflect on this, but we are told that when the servant heard their words, he bowed to the LORD. Then he brought out lavish gifts for Rebekah, her brother, and her mother (24:52–53). Apparently, the mother's clan is the more important here because the father is hardly mentioned. It should be noted that Rebekah is not reported as having any say in the matter. Her family made the decision and that was that.

The drama is not over, however. After eating with the family and spending the night, the servant of Abraham rose the next morning and announced his desire to leave to return to Abraham (24:54). The family wanted to delay Rebekah's departure for ten days (24:55), but Abraham's servant pressed for immediate departure (24:56). At this point the story reaches the most dramatic moment, for Rebekah's family leaves the decision to her (24:57)! Remember, this girl was probably no more than twelve to fourteen years old—that was the average age when girls were given in marriage at that time. There is no reason to assume that she had ever traveled far from Aram-naharaim, her home. She had no knowledge of what Canaan or, more importantly, Isaac, were like. And now to her was given the choice of yes or no that would determine the success of the servant's mission and the purpose of God that was to be served by it.

The narrator has taken fifty-seven verses to get us to this point. To the question of whether she will leave her family and go with Abraham's servant, Rebekah responded simply, "'I will'" (24:58). And in two more verses, after a blessing from Rebekah's family for her fertility and prosperity (24:60), Rebekah and her maids left for Canaan with Abraham's servant (24:61). The primary drama was over. Human decision had come together with divine purpose. Another step along the way had been accomplished.

## The Final Scene

While the suspense is over, the story is not yet finished. Rebekah and Isaac have not yet been united. So in the last verses of this chapter the narrator describes how their union came about. Isaac was living in the Negeb, the semidesert area somewhat south of where he had been when the servant departed on his mission (24:62). Isaac was taking a walk when the camels carrying Rebekah appeared (24:63). Rebekah slipped down from her camel and asked for the servant to identify the man coming to meet them (24:64–65). When told that it was Isaac, she veiled and covered herself with appropriate modesty and perhaps to provide visual symbols of her virginity and marriageability (24:65).

The servant reported to Isaac all that had happened (24:66). How much detail did he supply? Did he give the long version or a shorter one? We do not know, but as the narrator has already demonstrated, when it is time to conclude the story, the end comes quickly. The point of the story was to relate why and how Isaac was to have a bride. It concludes simply:

> Then Isaac brought her into his mother Sarah's tent. [Rebekah will replace the deceased Sarah as the matriarch of the clan.] He took Rebekah, and she became his wife; and he loved her. [The arranged marriage led to a relationship of loving care.] So Isaac was comforted after his mother's death. *(24:67)*

Such a lot packed into these few concluding verses!

## Conclusion

The story of Rebekah and her willing acceptance of the invitation to become the bride of Isaac is far more than an interesting narrative link in the unfolding of Genesis. It is a wonderfully crafted account that explores the way human decision and divine purpose are inseparably intertwined, and all by divine intent. In reading this account we are reminded that it matters to God how we approach life. Human decisions make a difference in the way the story unfolds and is told. What may often seem accidental may not be so at all. Only reflection on the happenings of our lives and interpretation in hindsight of their significance can lead to a trust in the guidance of God.

# Chapter Four
# Passing On the Promise

*A Study of Genesis 25:1–28:9*

## Introduction

The "history" of the divine promise received by Abraham and Sarah provides a unifying theme throughout Genesis 12–50. In this chapter we will consider the first crucial steps as the promise is passed from the first to the second and then the third generation of beneficiaries. As we have already seen, the people through whom God's story is acted out are extraordinarily "ordinary" in the sense that they have as many (or more) faults as strengths. That is why it is so easy for many of us to identify with Isaac, Rebekah, Esau, and Jacob, who are the people through whom the promise will be passed.

The story will be told in essentially three parts: the first concentrates on the birth of Esau and Jacob; the second, on Isaac and Rebekah in the court of Abimelech; and the third, on Isaac's "accidental" blessing of Jacob. It is not unfair to apply the term "dysfunctional" to the family portrayed in these stories. Again, that may be one of the reasons we find the account so engaging. We know what such families are like. Most of us have witnessed or experienced in our own families or in those of friends, at least to some degree, some of the intrigue and deception described in Genesis. The story of these biblical personages is the stuff of real life!

## Abraham's Last Days

After the narrator presented the powerful account of the choice of Rebekah to become Isaac's wife (Gen. 24), there were a few more details about Abraham that were important to record. According to tradition Abraham lived one hundred seventy-five years. The number is intended to emphasize the fullness of Abraham's life and is probably not to be taken literally (25:7–8). After his death, Abraham was buried by his first two sons, Ishmael and Isaac, in the cave of Machpelah alongside Sarah (25:9–10; see 23:17–20).

Isaac (whose mother was Sarah) and Ishmael (whose mother was Hagar) are the best known of Abraham's sons, but he had six others by another woman, Keturah, who is called both "wife" and "concubine" (25:1, 6). Among the grandchildren in this line of Abraham's offspring, the best known, perhaps, was Midian, who became the eponymous "father" of a nomadic tribe with whom Moses eventually became related (Exod. 2:15–22; 3:1; 18:27). Though Abraham sent Keturah and her children away (as he had Hagar and her son; see Gen. 21:8–21), he did give them gifts to provide for their livelihood (25:6).

Isaac and Rebekah and their sons become the focus of attention in the narrative, for it is through them that the divine promise will be passed. But before moving on, the narrator recorded the names of the descendants of Ishmael (25:12–18). God had promised Hagar that Ishmael would be "the father of twelve princes" (17:20), so the genealogy is presented. The Ishmaelites were Bedouin who moved about in the area mainly to the east and south of Palestine now known as Saudi Arabia. Today among Muslims Ishmael is of special importance because of his place in the Koran. Thus God's blessing of Ishmael, as promised to Hagar, was realized (21:18–21), and the story of the blessing of Isaac could proceed (25:11).

## Why Do I Live?

Pregnancy and birthing were dangerous in antiquity; mother and newborn were often at risk. In many parts of the world today they still are. A man may well celebrate a pregnancy, but it is a woman who has to endure it. (Surprisingly, the United States, among the industrialized nations, has the highest rate of infant mortality.)

So it was with Rebekah. She had married Isaac when he was forty and she was yet a young woman, probably in her early teens, living at home with her family (25:20; see 24:16). She did not become pregnant for many years, bearing her first child—that is, children, twins!—when Isaac was sixty (25:26). We are not told much of what went on during the twenty years before Rebekah bore her twins, but "barren" women carried a stigma in antiquity that was difficult to live with (see 16:1–6). Her circumstance was problematic enough to prompt Isaac to pray for her. Undoubtedly he was well pleased when she conceived (25:21).

Perhaps Rebekah was pleased as well, at least in the beginning, but her pregnancy became difficult; as the text puts it, "The children struggled together within her" (25:22). One child would have been difficult to carry at Rebekah's point in life, but to have two within her womb was trying indeed. Her discomfort was such that she put her feeling bluntly: "'If it is to be this way, why do I live?'" (25:22). When the twins were born, the first emerged with the second holding fast to the first's heel (25:26). Thus, the second was named "Jacob," which in Hebrew can mean either "he takes by the heel" or "he supplants" (25:26; 27:36). The firstborn was named "Esau" because of his red hair and ruddy complexion (25:25; but see also 25:30).

At this point it is important to consider the multiple uses of an ancient story. In answer to Rebekah's query about the purpose of life ("Why do I live?") amidst the struggle she endured in her pregnancy, the narrator placed an "answer" to a completely different question. In the world of the narrator there was concern for the relationship of two neighboring nations, Israel/Judah with Edom. Thus, the storyteller has inserted an oracle about this political issue as a supposed response to Rebekah's prayer (25:22). The response consisted of a divine word of declaration concerning the future of the twins within her. They each represented a nation, two peoples that would live separate from and in competition with the other, one stronger than the other, the younger prevailing over the elder (25:23). This was part of a tradition explaining the dominance of Israel over Edom in the history they shared. It would have been of little comfort to Rebekah, but to the people of Israel/Judah centuries later, these were words of assurance.

## Parental Favoritism

One of the rules of parenting is not to show favoritism to one child over another. Parents are encouraged to be objective, to treat each child equally, to emphasize the strengths of each child without comparing him or her with a sibling. This is the way it should be done. But real parenting does not always work out so neatly. In the case of Rebekah and Isaac with their two sons Esau and Jacob, the objective, equal-treatment-of-each model didn't even come close to being actualized.

As Esau and Jacob grew from childhood into adulthood, they developed distinctly different interests. Esau was the outdoor type, a skilled hunter. He liked to roam the countryside and bring home fresh game. Jacob, on the other hand, was a quiet person who preferred shepherd tents and domesticated flocks to the wild animals that Esau pursued. He liked staying inside out of the weather as opposed to tramping across the countryside. If there had been books in his day, he probably would have been an avid reader (25:27). And the text tells us simply and straightforwardly, "Isaac loved Esau, because he was fond of game; but Rebekah loved Jacob" (25:28). This contrast in the proclivities of the twins, coupled with the favoritism shown by their different parents, led to a major problem between the two that will be considered below. At this point it is enough to note that it was from the start part of a rivalry that grew across the years until it threatened to end in the murder of one by the other.

But before that crisis, consider one more aspect of the rivalry. One day while Esau was out hunting, Jacob was playing "chef of the day," preparing some hearty reddish-colored stew. Whether Jacob planned what happened beforehand or whether it was a coincidence that worked in Jacob's favor we do not know. Nevertheless, when Esau returned from his hunt and saw the stew, he desperately wanted to eat some of it (25:29–30). Rather than share his savory dish with his sibling with normal brotherly hospitality, Jacob seized an opportunity to gain a significant advantage over Esau. He offered the "starving" Esau a dish of stew in return for Esau's "birthright," his tradition-guaranteed right of inheritance as the firstborn (25:31).

The narrator is not kind to either of these men. On the one hand, the self-serving scheming of Jacob is pointed out by noting that he made his brother swear an oath giving Jacob his birthright before allowing Esau to eat (25:33). Then the narrator described Esau as wolfing down his food and walking away and thus "despising" his birthright (25:34). To care so little about one's heritage and inheritance was awful. To trick one's brother and manipulate him in a time of hunger and exhaustion was also despicable. Neither twin comes away looking too good.

## Promise and Deception as a Way of Life

Most readers of the Bible expect the major personages presented in the book to be honorable, admirable, exemplary people. With Isaac and Rebekah, at least in the stories we are considering here, such qualities seem startlingly absent.

The narrative continues with Isaac, who in the face of a severe famine takes Rebekah and their family to Gerar, a city governed by a Philistine, King Abimelech (26:1). At the outset of his journey the LORD appeared to Isaac and reaffirmed the promise of land, progeny, and prosperity that was given to Abraham and Sarah (26:3–5; see 12:2–3; 13:14–17; 15:5, 7, 18–21; 17:2–8; 22:17–18). This is the setting of the story.

There are several features of the story that raise immediate question. First, the exact location of Gerar is unknown. Second, so far as archaeology can determine, the Philistines did not enter Palestine until many centuries after the supposed time of Isaac and Rebekah. Third, a very similar story was told about Abraham and Sarah in Gerar (20:1–18; 21:22–34). But apart from issues of historicity, the story is valuable in offering insight into the way Isaac and Rebekah lived out their trust (or lack thereof) in the divine promise they had received. Like Abraham and Sarah before them, they did not demonstrate much confidence in the LORD God.

The ruse that they adopted was the same that Isaac's father and mother had tried. For fear he would be killed by the townsmen because of their lust for Rebekah, Isaac instructed her to say that she was his sister (26:7). They carried out their deception for some time until King Abimelech accidentally discovered their true relationship, that of husband and wife (26:8). The king was greatly distressed! Had one of his subjects had sexual relations with Rebekah—a married woman—great guilt would have fallen on Gerar (26:9–10). Isaac's "explanation" (26:9) certainly did not reflect the same level of ethical sensitivity as that displayed by his "pagan" host (26:10)! What's more, it indicated that Isaac lacked any strong conviction that the God who had given him the promise of progeny and prosperity would also provide necessary protection (26:3).

An unspecified period of time elapsed during which Isaac and his family, because of divine blessing, prospered greatly (26:12–13). He became so wealthy that he was perceived as a threat and was asked by King Abimelech to leave the area (26:14–16). After several moves prompted by disputes over water rights (26:17–25), Abimelech eventually came to Isaac and asked for a covenant to be established between them. In return for the generous way he and his people had treated Isaac, Abimelech asked Isaac to swear an oath of peace (26:26–30). This was done, and after a great feast sealing the agreement, Abimelech departed (26:31). That same day, water was found, and Isaac and his family settled in what then came to be called Beer-sheba, the "well of the oath" or the "well of seven" (26:33).

The inclusion of this story in the account makes at least two points clear. First, the human characters in the divine story are far from perfect, brave, moral folk. They are rather quite selfish at times and very untrusting of God's guidance. But at the same time, the second point that the story underscores is that the divine purpose is continued despite what the human characters may do. God's promise was going to be kept with or without the participation of the humans involved, but not in any fatalistic sort of way.

## The Grand Deceit

We have already noticed the way deception and parental favoritism marked the family life of Isaac and Rebekah. From almost the beginning Isaac had favored Esau whereas Rebekah had favored Jacob (25:28). The two of them, Isaac and Rebekah, practiced deception in their early days at Gerar (26:6–11). Then as Isaac "was old and his eyes were dim" (27:1), Rebekah fashioned an even greater act of deception.

Isaac, incapacitated by age and by increasingly bad sight, asked Esau to go out into the countryside to find some wild game for him to eat as prelude to Isaac's giving him his parental blessing (27:1–4). A father's "blessing" in antiquity was very significant, and once it was given it could not be retracted (27:35–37). It had all the weight of a sworn oath and was tantamount to a notarized will in our society, though it was not technically a legal statement. Usually the "blessing" was given to the oldest son, who in this story was Esau (27:1; but see also 24:60).

Rebekah overheard Isaac's conversation with Esau and launched the grand deceit (27:5). The plan was simple but bold. She instructed Jacob to select two "'choice kids'" for her to prepare as "'savory food'" that Jacob would serve to the nearly blind Isaac (27:5–10). Jacob initially resisted the plan for fear that the deception would fail because Esau was "'a hairy man'" and Jacob was "'a man of smooth skin'" (27:11). If Isaac touched him, he might think that Jacob was mocking him and then curse rather than bless him (27:12).

Rebekah, however, had already anticipated that possibility and had a plan to thwart it. She prepared the kids Jacob brought her. She then clothed Jacob in Esau's best clothes. In addition, she put the "skins of the kids on his [Jacob's] hands and on the smooth part of his neck," so if Isaac touched Jacob he would mistake him for Esau (27:14–17). Rebekah was so sure of her plan that she was willing to risk and bear any curse that might come their way (27:13).

The narrator does a splendid job of pulling the hearers/readers into the story. Carefully we witness the drama of the aged, nearly blind Isaac's receiving Jacob. Isaac was not sure of who had drawn near his bedside. To his query about identity, Jacob identified himself as "'Esau your firstborn'" (27:19). Clearly he had joined his mother in the grand deceit. Isaac was still unconvinced; how could Esau so quickly have found game and been able to prepare it? He then asked Jacob to come near so that he could "'feel'" him to make certain he was really Esau (27:20–21). On touching Jacob Isaac commented, "'The voice is Jacob's voice, but the hands are the hands of Esau'" (27:22). Isaac's uncertainty continued, however, until even after he had eaten. He had Jacob come near, and he kissed him so that he could get as close as possible. When Isaac "smelled the smell of his garments," Esau's clothes, only then was Isaac convinced (27:24–27). The coveted parental blessing then followed (27:28–29). The grand deceit was successful!

The drama, however, was far from over. No sooner had Jacob left his father's bedside when Esau proudly and happily brought the game he had prepared to his father (27:30–31). Isaac was confused. Who had just been with him? Who had just served him a fine meal? Who was this who now drew near with another fine-smelling meal? Whom had he just blessed? Isaac asked, "'Who are you?'" And Esau replied, "'I am your firstborn son, Esau'" (27:32–33). As it dawned on Esau what had happened, he uttered an "exceedingly great and bitter cry" and pled for Isaac to bless him as well (27:34).

But there could be no "second" blessing. Jacob had acted deceitfully and had "taken away" Esau's blessing (27:35). Though Esau begged for a blessing (27:36, 38), there was none (27:37). Jacob, the "supplanter" (25:26), had first taken Esau's birthright (25:29–34); now he had taken away Esau's blessing (27:36). All Esau could do was weep (27:38) and hate (27:41)!

## The Blessings

While the story of Jacob's deceptive acquisition of Isaac's parental blessing emphasized *one* blessing, the account as we have it actually preserves several. The first is presented in conjunction with the meal that Rebekah prepared and Jacob served to Isaac (27:27–29). Two major emphases are present: fertility/prosperity and dominion.

The agricultural setting is obvious from the nature of the blessing: ample rain ("'the dew of heaven'"), the fecundity ("'fatness'") of the earth, and "'plenty of grain and wine'" (27:28). Isaac's blessing promised that the land that Jacob would have, a land described much later as a land flowing with "milk and honey" (Num. 13:27; Deut. 31:20), would be rich and fertile.

The blessing also had a political dimension. How broadly the dominion promised was to extend is not clear. Those who would bow down to Jacob, acknowledging his rule, included his "'brothers'" and "'mother's sons,'" but "'peoples'" and "'nations'" are also mentioned (27:29). The latter terms may be inclusive of the references to brothers and sons (27:37). At least the blessing envisions subjugation of some level or another of the peoples surrounding Jacob/Israel. Additionally there is a two-fold declaration about acknowledging Jacob's dominion: those who resist and curse Jacob will be cursed; but those who bless Jacob will themselves be blessed (27:29; see 12:3).

A second blessing was given to Jacob. Rebekah learned that Esau threatened to kill his brother (27:41–42). That plus her fear that Jacob might marry one of the Hittites as had his brother (26:34–35; 27:46) prompted her to arrange for Jacob to go to her family in Paddan-aram (28:1–5). Jacob's departure was necessary both to escape the fury of his brother (27:41–45) and to find a suitable bride among their kinfolk there. As Jacob prepared to leave, Isaac called him in and charged him to go north to find a proper bride (28:1). Then he blessed Jacob (again), praying that God would make him "'fruitful and numerous'" so as to become "'a company of peoples'" (28:3). Further, Isaac specifically linked his blessing with the blessing that Abraham had received, adding the assurance of possession of land to the prayer for fertility (28:4; see 12:2–3; 13:15–17; 15:5, 7, 18–21; 17:2–8; 22:17–18).

A word is necessary here about Rebekah's behavior. From the outset of her appearance in this account she is portrayed as self-confident and "assertive" (see the previous chapter). She had watched over her boys from their birth to their young adulthood. She certainly favored Jacob (25:28) and worked to make things better for him (27:5–17), but she had some care for Esau as well. She acted in such a way that Esau would have time to come to his own senses and resolve his hate for his brother. She did not want to risk Jacob's being killed by Esau, but she also did not want to see Esau stoned to death for the murder of his brother, for that would have been his punishment. As she says, "'Why should I lose both of you in one day?'" (27:45). Even though she had her favorite, she was still a mother. Most of the time, our motives and actions are tangled and multifaceted. Moral and ethical "purity" is a rare commodity.

## Esau the Slighted One

Esau certainly got the short end of the stick in this account. Yes, he brought some of it on himself with his bravado and his assumptions about his "rights" as firstborn and favorite of his father (25:27, 30–34). Nonetheless, he was manipulated and made the victim of deception by his mother and his brother (25:33–34; 27:34–38). He then married outside the clan and thereby further lowered himself in the eyes of his mother (26:34–35; 28:6–9).

Isaac did "bless" Esau, but it was quite ambiguous. It is unclear whether Esau was to be with or without the "'fatness of the earth'" and the "'dew of heaven'" (27:39). The Hebrew is simply unclear! He was to live by the sword and have a troubled future with his brother (27:40). "Blessed"? Maybe so, but his "blessing" was certainly not as positive as that bestowed on Jacob.

This glimpse into the relationship of these twins, Jacob and Esau, allows us a perspective on something quite bigger that the narrator had in mind. Part of what we are learning has to do with the political realities in the writer's world. Jacob was the eponymous head of the people Israel. Esau was the traditional progenitor of Edom (see 36:1–43). These two nations wrestled throughout the tenth to the sixth centuries, usually with Israel (Jacob) holding the upper hand. Thus, behind this story of two brothers is another narrative about two nations in which Israel as a people is the winner over its "brother," the Edomites.

## Conclusion

We have considered texts that describe a very human struggle within a family, a rather dysfunctional family if the facts be known. A mother and father are divided in their regard for their sons. Two brothers are pictured in sometimes brutal competition with each other for the attention of their parents. Esau and Jacob each angled for dominance over the other, signified in gaining the father's blessing. Lurking just under the surface was a shadow of the national histories of two people, the Israelites and the Edomites. The amazing point that ties the whole narrative together is that the promise of God, first to Abraham and Sarah and then to Isaac and Rebekah, was being passed from one generation to the next. The divine purpose was being worked out but, as always, in a very particular manner that can at times seem unfair. Jacob received the promise; Esau did not!

# Chapter Five

# Mystery Surrounds the Ordinary

*A Study of Genesis 28:10–32:32*

## Introduction

The story of Jacob's journey into manhood—as he becomes a husband and father in a land far removed from that of his upbringing—is gripping. There is all the drama and intrigue we have come to expect when Jacob is on the scene: duplicity, competition, and conflict. At the same time, however, the story is quite ordinary, a very human account of people who sound very real if not quite modern. In most of the narrative there is no mention of direct encounters with God; indeed, only at the beginning and end of Jacob's odyssey are there extraordinary accounts of such experiences of the divine. Nevertheless, the reader/hearer knows all along that God is very attentive to what is unfolding. God's providential care is once again being demonstrated in and through the mundane events of Jacob's life.

## Jacob's Mysterious Dream

Most of the story about Jacob is very "secular," concerned with economic matters and families, not things that most people might call "religious." But it doesn't begin that way. In the previous chapter we considered the enmity that had developed between Jacob and Esau, primarily because of the deception that had brought Isaac's blessing to Jacob rather than to Esau, the elder brother and expected recipient. Because Jacob was facing a tense and threatening situation, Rebekah instructed him to leave and travel northward to find refuge, and possibly a wife, among Rebekah's family in Haran, located in the region of Paddam-aram in northwest Mesopotamia (28:10; see also 27:43–45; 28:2). Jacob followed the main road north that led from Beer-sheba through the hill country by way of Hebron and on to Shechem, the reverse of the path his ancestors Abraham and Sarah had taken.

What began as a "routine" trip (if you can call a flight from possible murder routine) turned into something strange and mysterious. Jacob stopped at Luz (28:19), a place that came to be named Bethel because of what happened to him there. He had apparently traveled for several days before reaching Luz because it was located about seventy miles from Beer-sheba, a few miles north of modern Jerusalem. We might be able to travel that distance today in a few hours, but Jacob did not have an auto or a highway to ease his travel. As darkness came, Jacob settled down for a normal night on the road. He made his bed using a stone as a sort of pillow (28:11). So far as we are told, Jacob had no inkling of anything unusual about the place and certainly no preparation for what was to happen.

During the night Jacob had a dream. Many modern people scoff at the idea that dreams have any significance for the way one might go about life although many others consider dreams a window into the soul if not into the eternal. In Jacob's time people believed dreams were one way that deities communicated with mortals. The Bible reports a number of persons who had significant dreams (e.g., Joseph in Gen. 37:5–7, 9; Daniel in Dan. 7:1 ff.; and Joseph in Matt. 2:13). Sometimes, however, dreams in antiquity were challenged as an untrustworthy means of divine communication (Jer. 23:28; 29:8–9). Nonetheless, for the first hearers of Jacob's story there would have been no question that a dream had to be taken seriously.

Jacob dreamed that he saw a "ladder" connecting the earth with the heavens (28:12). It is better to think of this "ladder" more like a ramp that allowed ascent to and descent from the realm of the divine. In ancient Mesopotamia the ziggurat was a regular type of temple consisting of a pyramid-like structure around which wound an external ramp that led to the top where a shrine was located. On this ramp, or ladder, Jacob saw that innumerable "angels of God were ascending and descending on it" (28:12). Clearly he was on holy ground!

What is even more significant, however, is that none of these heavenly messengers addressed Jacob at all. Rather, the text declares that the LORD himself spoke to Jacob with a life-defining message. The promise that had been communicated to Jacob by Isaac in the form of a parental blessing (28:3–4) was now spoken by the LORD, "'the God of Abraham your father and the God of Isaac'"

(28:13)! God intended for Jacob and his numerous offspring to have the land on which Jacob lay (28:13–14). The divine promise that had first been given to Abraham and Sarah was now given to Jacob quite apart from his father Isaac's blessing. Moreover, as Jacob was on the verge of leaving this special place and his homeland, God promised to accompany him, ensuring his safety and success until Jacob returned (28:15). The authority for this communication rested not with any of the angels that Jacob saw; no, it was directly from the LORD God.

## Jacob's Response

When Jacob awoke, he knew he had slept in an awesome place (28:16)! Had he known he was in such a place, he might not have spent the night there. With a play on a Hebrew word that denotes "fear" or "awe," Jacob is said to be "afraid" in the "awesome" place (28:17). He then interpreted his own experience as having been in the "'house of God'" (in Hebrew *Beth-el*) at the very "'gate of heaven'" (28:17). What's more, he named the place "Bethel" in remembrance of his encounter with God (28:19), and he took the stone on which he slept, erected it on the spot as a pillar, and anointed it with oil to mark its special character (28:18). (Bethel became a major sanctuary in the centuries to come. It was attacked and sacked by members of the "house of Joseph" in the eleventh century [Judg. 1:22–26], and Samuel made at least yearly visits to the center [1 Sam. 7:16]. When the kingdom of David and Solomon split apart in the tenth century, Jeroboam I, the first king of the northern kingdom, Israel, designated Bethel as the site of one of his two royal sanctuaries [1 Kgs. 12:26–33].)

Jacob did not stop with erecting a pillar and designating the place "'house of God.'" He also made a vow, the wording of which is somewhat misleading in English. God had already promised to be with Jacob wherever he went (28:15), so for Jacob to begin with the words "'If God will be with me . . .'" (28:20) sounds as though Jacob was bargaining with God. That was not the intent. The point was that Jacob was repeating the vows that God had already made to him as Jacob's way of recognizing them and making them his own. He expected God's presence in his continuing journey, and he expected to return one day (28:20–22). Further, Jacob vowed to present God a tithe, one tenth, of all the blessings he anticipated from God (28:22). Tithing was widely practiced in Mesopotamia and became part of the biblical code (see Deut. 14:22–29). With his vow Jacob affirmed his relationship with God and the sanctity of the shrine that he constructed at the "'gate of heaven,'" the "'house of God.'"

Jacob's experience is noteworthy on many accounts. Perhaps one of the most important is what it says about the mobility of God. In the ancient world, and still for many today, God is sought at specific places, particular established shrines. Jacob, in fact, fashioned such a sanctuary at Bethel. But the word he received in his dream assured him that God was going to travel with him wherever he went. That was a new idea in the middle of the second millennium BCE, when deities were associated with fixed places. Whenever a god or goddess encountered a person, it was local, at a specific holy place. Jacob's dream declared a different way for the divine presence to be known. God was going to be Jacob's "traveling companion." Centuries later when the people of God were scattered around the Middle East by famine and war, the theology of a "mobile" God became all the more important. Clearly Christians assume it, even though we sometimes become too attached to our church buildings.

## Jacob Meets His Match

After his foray into the mysterious at Bethel, Jacob resumed his trek to the north in search of Rebekah's brother Laban. Clearly we are back in the realm of the ordinary; another day in the life of a guy seeking to secure his life and his future. We are not told how long Jacob traveled to reach the territory of the "people of the east" (29:1), but several hundred miles by foot is not an overnight hike.

Jacob came upon a group of shepherds with their flocks waiting near a well where they intended to water their sheep. As was their custom, they waited until all the flocks were gathered before they opened the well (29:2–3). Jacob asked where they were from. When they said, "Haran," his ears perked up. He asked if they knew Laban, and sure enough, they did (29:4–5). As Jacob was inquiring about the well-being of Laban, a flock of Laban's sheep was approaching, tended by Laban's daughter Rachel. After Rachel brought her sheep near, the well was opened, and all the animals were watered (29:6–8).

Jacob was ecstatic when he realized that Rachel was Laban's daughter. He immediately began helping with the watering of the flocks. He "kissed" Rachel—not a romantic kiss but a familial kiss of greeting (see 29:13; Exod. 4:27; Ruth 1:9, 14)—and wept for joy (29:10–11). When she learned that Jacob was a kinsman, she immediately went and brought her father, Laban, to meet him. Therein began a relationship between Jacob and the family of Laban that was to last for a number of years (29:12–14).

Esau had not been a match for Jacob in terms of the capacity to manipulate a situation, but Laban was! After receiving the hospitality of his kinsman for a month (29:14), Jacob was approached by Laban to determine a more permanent arrangement. Laban asked, "'Because you are my kinsman, should you therefore serve me for nothing? Tell me, what shall your wages be?'"(29:15). While this sounded simply like a polite question, Laban was much too devious for that and had every intention of getting the most he could from Jacob.

Laban had two daughters; the older was named Leah, and the younger, Rachel. Jacob had fallen in love with the "graceful and beautiful" Rachel almost immediately. So he asked for her to be his bride in return for seven years of service to Laban (29:16–18). Laban agreed, and Jacob began his years of service (29:19–21). This arrangement may seem strange to us, but in the ancient world of Mesopotamia it was common practice for the family of a young woman to be given money or some expensive gift as part of a marriage contract. In Jacob's case, he himself had to pay the bride money the only way he could, by service.

At the end of his seven years Jacob, according to their agreement, prepared to marry Rachel. Laban invited all the people to a great feast to celebrate the marriage. Then Laban turned the tables on Jacob, who himself had more than once acted the role of the great deceiver. Laban brought Leah, his older daughter, to Jacob (who may not have been totally sober). Jacob, thinking she was Rachel, "went in to her," or in other words, he sexually consummated his marriage to her (29:23–25). When Jacob awoke and saw Leah beside him, he was aghast! He knew he had been deceived by Laban (29:25)! When he confronted Laban, Laban's reply no doubt brought grins to the first audience as they saw the twist being made on Jacob. Laban said simply, "'This is not done in our country—giving the younger before the firstborn'" (29:26). Jacob by deception had received what should have gone to his older brother, the firstborn, but such was not to be the case with Laban's daughters!

A "solution" was worked out, one that initially was to Laban's advantage. Jacob completed the week-long wedding ritual with Leah. Rachel then was given to him as a second wife, and "Jacob went in to Rachel also" (29:30). Jacob agreed to serve Laban seven more years as the "price" for Rachel (29:27). For a man to have several wives was not considered inappropriate at the time; in fact, two additional women came into Jacob's family: Zilpah, Leah's maid, and Bilhah, Rachel's maid (29:24, 29). The narrator added a significant footnote: Jacob loved Rachel more than he loved Leah (29:30).

## Jacob's Expanding Family

Jacob's marriages—two in two weeks—were unusual in the deceptive way they came about. Nonetheless, they were clearly part of the ordinary world of human affairs. Likewise, the birth of children was to be expected. Leah was the first to get pregnant. Because she was keenly aware of Jacob's greater love for Rachel, she gave names symbolic of her distress to each of the four sons she bore. Reuben, the firstborn's name, meant "See, a son," reflecting Leah's hope that Jacob would love her more because she bore him a son (29:32). Three more sons were born: Simeon (God has heard), Levi (joined to me), and Judah (praise the Lord). Then, the text tells us, Leah ceased bearing (29:33–35).

Meanwhile, in a story reminiscent of Sarah's experience (16:1), Rachel was barren (30:1). Jacob and Rachel each blamed the other for Rachel's failure to conceive. Jacob considered Rachel's childlessness the direct work of God, an attitude that was no doubt extremely painful to Rachel (30:2). For Rachel, not only was her relationship with Jacob an issue, but her self-worth as well, since her society considered childbearing the primary vocation for a woman. Eventually Rachel was "remembered" by God. She bore a son she named Joseph, saying, "'May the LORD add to me another son!'" (30:22–24).

There were other children born into Jacob's family. Leah later bore Issachar, Zebulun, and one daughter, Dinah (30:16–21). Zilpah, Leah's maid, bore two sons, Gad and Asher (30:10–13). Likewise, Rachel's maid, Bilhah, bore Dan and Naphtali (30:3–8).

Through all the drama of the numerous children conceived and born to Jacob and his four wives, the ordinary is juxtaposed to the extraordinary. God's involvement is a rather shadowed affair, for there are no scenes of direct encounter between God and the humans at the center of the story. Yet God is not totally absent either, remaining mysteriously there but not there.

## Jacob's Success and Laban's Distress

After Joseph's birth, Jacob asked to be allowed to take his family and return to his own country (30:25–26). Laban was reluctant to have Jacob leave, both because of the prosperity that Jacob had brought (30:27) and because of his daughters and numerous grandchildren that would go with him. So, the ever-conniving Laban offered a deal to the equally crafty Jacob for Jacob's continuing service. As his wages, Jacob was allowed to remove from Laban's flock every "speckled and spotted sheep and every black lamb, and the spotted and speckled among the goats" (30:31–32). These animals were to be the start of Jacob's flocks. Laban enthusiastically agreed (30:34), but that very day had all the agreed-on stock removed and taken three days' journey away from where Jacob was pasturing the rest of Laban's flock (30:35–36).

Jacob, however, was not to be cheated once again by his father-in-law. He adopted a practice that folklore held effective. He manipulated the breeding of the flocks so that more and strong animals of the kind that Jacob could claim were produced (30:37–42). As the text summarizes, "Thus the man [Jacob] grew exceedingly rich, and had large flocks, and male and female slaves, and camels and donkeys" (30:43). Laban's trickery had backfired on him.

## Jacob's Flight

Once again Jacob found himself in a conflict with members of the family. Laban's sons and Laban himself thought that Jacob had somehow robbed them of their wealth (31:1–2). Enter unexpectedly the LORD, with a word to Jacob: "'Return to the land of your ancestors and to your kindred, and I will be with you'" (31:3).

Jacob called his wives to him and explained what had happened, how he had been instructed by God about how to increase his flocks. Laban had repeatedly changed Jacob's agreed-on wages, but God had enabled Jacob to succeed (31:7–9). In response to his explanations, Leah and Rachel stated their own frustrations with their father's behavior. They were prepared to go with Jacob (31:14–16). Immediately, Jacob and the whole family headed south for the land of Canaan (31:17–18).

Laban, of course, learned of Jacob's departure and set out in hot pursuit, being warned by God, however, to take care with the way he dealt with Jacob (31:19–24). He overtook Jacob and his entourage seven days later and chastised Jacob for deceiving him by leaving without telling him, thereby depriving him of giving them a suitable send-off (31:25–29). What's more, he charged Jacob with stealing Laban's household gods (31:30), idols representing deities that were important to Laban. Rachel, unknown to Jacob, had indeed taken them (31:19). A humorous scene follows with Laban vainly searching for his idols, not realizing that his menstruating daughter, Rachel, has them in the camel saddle she is sitting on (31:35). So not only were the household idols stolen; they were also "soiled" by contact with a woman during her period! The satire was delightful!

More could be said. Jacob and Laban came to a settlement recognizing that Jacob had dealt fairly with Laban (31:36–42). They made a covenant that in effect pledged their mutual intention to leave the other alone and asked God to watch over them to assure that neither violated the agreement (31:43–54). Afterward, Laban said good-bye to his daughters and grandchildren and returned to his home (31:55).

## Jacob Becomes Israel

After Laban had departed, Jacob continued his journey south. In anticipation of meeting his brother, Esau, Jacob sent messengers ahead alerting Esau of Jacob's return (32:3). The messengers brought back word that Esau was coming to meet Jacob, accompanied by four hundred men (32:6). This news prompted Jacob, in distress, to divide the "people that were with him, and the flocks and herds and camels" so that if Esau were to destroy one group, the other might escape (32:7–8). Then he prayed to God, reminding the LORD that Jacob had started south because of the divine word that had come to him (32:9–10; see 31:3). Jacob asked for divine protection and deliverance from Esau and reminded God of God's promise of protection, not because of Jacob's faithfulness but because of the divine commitment to Abraham and Isaac before him (32:11–12). He then sent ahead a large gift intended to appease Esau (32:13–21). Jacob next sent his two wives, two maids, and his eleven "children" (the writer did not count his daughter Dinah, and Benjamin had not yet been born [35:16–18]), with everything that was still with him, across the ford of the Jabbok River (32:22–23).

The Jabbok flows into the Jordan River about twenty miles north of the Dead Sea. It is one of the natural east-west points of passage from or into the land of Canaan. When Jacob was there alone, a "man" attacked and wrestled with him until dawn (32:24). Before the episode is over the audience is led to realize that this is no ordinary mortal; it is God in the form of a human being (32:28–30)! This passage is a strange and mysterious one that may originally have been about an unknown river deity that guarded the ford, but here it has been transformed into a story about the continuing struggle between humans and God as they go through life.

Neither Jacob nor his initially unknown assailant, however, was able to achieve a decisive victory. Eventually the "man" struck Jacob "on the hip socket" (32:25; the exact meaning of the Hebrew word translated "hip socket" is unknown) and rendered Jacob somewhat lame (32:31). Jacob sought to learn the name of the one with whom he wrestled (32:29), but his request was denied. Nonetheless, the "man" (God) did bless Jacob, giving him a new name, "Israel," because, as the narrator puts it, "'You have striven with God and with humans, and have prevailed'" (32:28; but see 35:10). Jacob named the place "Peniel" (also spelled "Penuel" in the same passage) which means "face of God" for, as he said, "'I have seen God face to face, and yet my life is preserved'" (32:30; but see Exod. 33:20). Thus as Jacob prepared to reenter the land of Canaan, the land promised to Abraham and Isaac, he did so in full awareness of God's presence with him. He was injured in his struggle with the divine, but he was also assured that God had not and would not abandon him; God's presence as offered in the promise continued.

## Conclusion

Jacob's story is ordinary in most respects. As a young man he struck out on his own to find a wife and make a livelihood. In his case the beginning was somewhat clouded because of conflict with his brother and father. He acquired a wife—in fact several—and became quite well-to-do. Again, there are some unusual aspects to the story, but it is still that of happenings in the ordinary world. Bracketing this ordinary life, however, are two quite extraordinary accounts of encounters with God. Jacob is assured in the first of God's commitment to go with him into the unknown. Likewise, in the second God's continuing presence is made vivid to Jacob in a strange manner uncommon to the experience of most of us: by Jacob's wrestling to a draw with the Almighty. Mystery indeed surrounds the ordinary!

# Chapter Six

# Loose Ends

## A Study of Genesis 33:1–36:43

### Introduction

The book of Genesis was constructed from many different sources of tradition. Various sections—like the stories about Jacob and Laban we considered in the previous chapter—may have been passed along separately before they were brought together into what we now call Genesis. The various pieces fit together sometimes closely and sometimes only loosely. In this lesson we are going to examine several different traditions. The ones dealing with Jacob and Esau clearly continue the story begun back in chapter 28, but the account of Dinah's rape and Jacob's second visit to Bethel do not fit so tightly. Nonetheless, the writer or writers of Genesis believed these to be important enough to warrant preservation. Thus they are placed here before what will be one of the longest and best constructed bodies of tradition in the book (Gen. 37–50), which will be the subject of chapter 7, with its focus on the Joseph stories.

## Jacob and Esau Reunited

As Jacob prepared to leave Penuel, he saw Esau with four hundred men approaching (33:1). Not knowing Esau's intent, Jacob divided up his entourage so that his people could flee more easily if that was necessary. He placed the maids with their children at the front, followed by Leah and her children. Rachel and Joseph were in the back. Jacob went ahead to meet Esau (33:1–3). To Jacob's astonishment, Esau ran to him, embraced him, and kissed him; and they both wept (33:4). Esau then met Jacob's family, his wives and all his children (33:5–7).

Esau inquired about all the gifts sent to him by Jacob (33:8; see 32:16–21). What were they for? Jacob "explained" that he had offered the gifts in hopes of receiving Esau's "favor" (33:8). "Favor" is a term in Hebrew that is frequently used to indicate that someone has shown "acceptance" of another or has shown "kindness" when it was not necessary to do so. For Esau to grant favor to Jacob was, in a sense, to indicate forgiveness. With utmost politeness—clearly shown in the choice of Hebrew terms employed but not as obvious in translation—Jacob asked for Esau to accept Jacob's gift as a sign of Esau's favor (33:8). In his "bargaining" Jacob also indicated that he understood Esau's warm welcome as already an extension of Esau's favor to him (33:10; a different Hebrew word is used here that means "to be pleased with" or "to accept favorably"). The clear affirmation of this favor and the sign of reconciliation accomplished were for Esau to accept Jacob's gift, and he did (33:11).

The episode ends with Esau and Jacob parting ways; Esau departs to Seir (Edom), and Jacob, to Succoth (33:16–17) and eventually on to Shechem, where he will buy some land (33:18–20). Esau offered to travel with Jacob or at least to leave some of his people to help Jacob and his family in their continuing journey (33:12, 15). Jacob, however, declined, saying that his family and flocks would necessarily have to travel more slowly (33:13–14). Further he asked, "'Why should my lord be so kind to me?'" (33:15), revealing a lot about the underlying situation.

Jacob addressed his brother as "'lord,'" indicating Jacob's sense of a still-present power differential that rested with his brother. What's more, the term translated "kind" is once again the word translated earlier as "favor." Jacob apparently did not want to be in any more debt to his brother or dependent on his hospitality more than necessary. From Jacob's point of view, he had evened the score. The brothers could be "nice" to one another now, but neither needed to depend on the other's "favor."

## Meaning at Several Levels

Modern readers listen to the stories of Jacob and Esau as interesting tales about long-ago times. There are parallels, on occasion, with life today—after all, we all share much as human beings—but these stories do not speak, for the most part, to our ongoing history. To those who first received these traditions, however, more was being said than may meet our eyes.

As indicated in the previous chapter, Esau was considered to be the eponymous "father" of the Edomites, a people who occupied an area south of the Dead Sea on both sides of the Arabah, clear to the Gulf of Aqaba or Elath. The extended genealogy of Esau's family testifies to this (36:1–43). Likewise, Jacob was the eponymous head of the Israelites, thus the extended description of the birth of all Jacob's children (29:31–30:24; 35:16–18). Jacob's family eventually occupied the land west of the Jordan River, from Beer-sheba in the south to the southern slopes of Lebanon. These two peoples, the Israelites and Edomites, lived as neighbors into the fifth century BCE, sometimes with one in ascendancy and sometimes with the other exercising more influence in the region.

Depending on the historical circumstances, the Edomites were considered as more or less "hostile" relatives by those who preserved these stories in Genesis many centuries after the events described. Later Israelites knew from other traditions that the Edomites had refused permission for Moses and the group he led to pass through their land (Num. 20:14–21). They knew that King David during his reign (roughly 1000–960 BCE) conquered and occupied Edom for a significant period (2 Sam. 8:13–14). Somewhat later, during the reign of Judah's King Jehoram (850–843 BCE), Edom revolted against Judah and gained independence for about sixty years (2 Kgs. 8:20–22). Judah was able to regain control until the time of Judah's King Ahaz (742–725 BCE), when Edom defeated Judah and once and for all ended Judean hegemony (2 Kgs. 16:6; 2 Chr. 28:17). Later readers/hearers knew these things!

The point of this brief historical excursion is that what may seem to the modern reader as quaint or entertaining stories have sometimes meant much more to earlier audiences. The suspicion that "Esau" might yet try to take revenge against "Jacob" was always there. The prophets record some of the ongoing distrust in their oracles (see Jer. 49:7–22; Ezek. 25:12–14; Amos 1:11–12; Obad. 1–14). Thus the peace between Jacob and Esau was always seen as somewhat fragile and perhaps a little precarious, and the text was heard with real historical memory.

## The Rape of Dinah

The narrative link between chapters 33 and 34 is the note that Jacob and his family made it "safely," all in one piece, whole (the Hebrew word translated "safely" is from the same root as *shalom,* which means "wholeness," "peace") to Shechem (33:18). Shechem was the place that Abraham and Sarah had first stopped when they entered the land of Canaan (12:6). In Shechem lived Hamor, who had several sons, one of whom was named Shechem. Jacob purchased land from Hamor's sons and settled his family there in the hill country (33:19). Jacob erected an altar and called it El-Elohe-Israel (33:20). While this may seem harmless, the name can be heard to make a rather bold claim, namely, that the god "El" widely worshiped among the Canaanites was in fact the "God of Israel," something that few Canaanites might have been willing to acknowledge. From this rather "factual," bland beginning, the story that then unfolds is one of brutality and deception, two marks we have already noticed too often among the traditions in Genesis.

Apparently Jacob's clan was getting settled down in their new home in Shechem. Dinah, Jacob's only named daughter, whose mother was Leah (30:21), went to visit some of the Canaanite women who lived nearby (34:1). Shechem, son of Hamor, saw Dinah and was overcome with lust. Whether this was the first time Shechem the Hivite (or Canaanite) had seen her seems unlikely, but the text does not tell us that. Whatever the case may be, Shechem "seized her and lay with her by force" (34:2). He raped Dinah!

Then, and quite unexpectedly, the text reports that Shechem's "soul was drawn to Dinah," and "he loved the girl, and spoke tenderly to her" (34:3). Recognizing that what he had done was wrong, Shechem asked his father to help right the wrong by arranging for Dinah to become his wife (34:4). "'Get me this girl'" may sound harsh to modern ears, but it is typical language used for those making arranged marriages (see 24:3, 37–40).

The story at this point develops along two parallel but different lines aimed at distinctly different outcomes. First there is the reaction of Dinah's father and brothers when they learned of her rape. Jacob was alone when he received the news that "Shechem had defiled his daughter Dinah," so he kept his cool ("held his peace") and waited for his sons to return (34:5). When the brothers heard what had happened, they went ballistic ("were indignant and very angry") and immediately began thinking about how to right the "outrage in Israel" that Dinah's rape represented to them (34:7).

Parallel to the brothers' vehement anger was the action by Shechem's father, Hamor. He immediately went out to the field to find Jacob and to try to make things right (34:6). He did not deny or try to make excuse for Shechem's action, but he insisted that Shechem, in fact, loved Dinah and wanted her to be his wife (34:8). Hamor urged Jacob and his brothers to interact positively with the people of the city, giving and taking in marriage, trading and buying property (34:9–10). Shechem asked Jacob and her brothers to allow him to marry Dinah, which seems to attest to the sincerity of his love for her. Whatever conditions they wanted to set were agreeable to Shechem (34:11–12).

Such a proposal may seem out of line to us, but it was totally in accord with the legal codes of the ancient Near East (including Israel's). If a man raped an unbetrothed (or unengaged) virgin, the "legal" and proper way to right the wrong was for that man to pay the bride-price to the woman's father, marry the woman, and agree never to divorce her (see Exod. 22:16–17; Deut. 22:28–29). This was the context in which Dinah's future was considered.

In contrast to the "legal" and positive efforts of Hamor and Shechem to correct a terrible wrong, Jacob's sons responded "deceitfully" or "treacherously" (the Hebrew word carries both connotations) (34:13). It seems, perhaps, that they were more concerned about "an outrage in Israel" (34:7), or somehow disgracing themselves (34:14), than caring for their sister. After all, Shechem had willingly come forward to make restitution as best he could and had announced his love for Dinah. But the brothers set a condition: only if all the non-Israelite men in the city were circumcised could Dinah become Shechem's wife. Then, and only then, might other women be given in marriage as well (34:14–17).

Hamor and Shechem were "pleased" by the offer and accepted the terms. They did so in good faith not knowing (as we the readers do) that it was "deceitful" (34:18; see 34:13). Thus they persuaded the other men in the community also to be circumcised. They pointed out that the land was large enough for the Shechemites and the Israelites to live together. They would trade together and intermarry, and as Hamor noted, "Will not their livestock, their property, and all their animals be ours?" After all, the Shechemites were clearly the majority population and the Israelites the minority. So, all the Shechemite men agreed to be circumcised (34:18–24).

Of course, the story did not end with everyone living together happily ever after. While the Shechemite men were still painfully recovering from their circumcision, Simeon and Levi, Dinah's brothers, snuck into the city and killed all the men (34:25). They also forcibly took Dinah out of Shechem's house (34:26). The text does not indicate Dinah's reaction to all the violence, but there is also no suggestion that she was being held against her will by Shechem. Next the sons of Jacob (the RSV says "other sons," which would exclude Levi and Simeon, but the term "other" is not in the Hebrew text) pillaged the city, taking all their wealth, livestock, and women and children (34:27–29).

Jacob was greatly displeased by what his sons had done. They claimed that it was a matter of revenging the honor of their sister, who had been defiled and "'treated like a whore'" (34:27, 31). But Dinah was not a whore; she had not sold herself to Shechem, and everyone knew that. She had been raped and the proper legal act of restitution had been made. Shechem had willingly married Dinah. Moreover, the Shechemites had willingly agreed to be circumcised. Jacob recognized what his sons had done and understood the long-term consequences of their treacherous action. He castigated them, especially Simeon and Levi, for their act. To gain "honor" and wealth for themselves they had put the whole clan into potential danger. The Israelites were few in number relative to the Canaanites. Should the people of the land decide to join together, they could easily overwhelm the Israelites (34:30).

The story was not remembered as a guide for action, except in the sense of "this was no way to act"! But it did help explain why certain "tribes" later had their place in the "family order." In a poem known as "Jacob's Last Words to his Sons" (Gen. 49:1–28), Jacob announced what he believed would happen to his various children in the future. Simeon and Levi were cursed for their anger and wrath, for their cruelty. They were not to have any place in the family council. They were to be divided and scattered among the rest of Israel (49:5–7). In the course of time Simeon did fade from any recognizable identity, and Levi was spread throughout the various clans and cities.

The Canaanites did resist the Israelites with distrust and continued as suspicious "neighbors" through Israel's later national history. The story of the brutal revenge prompted by the rape of Dinah served as a reminder of how easily relationships with neighboring people can go wrong. Shechem certainly committed a heinous act, but Simeon and Levi did so as well. This story provided a study in how retaliation is seldom a helpful response, a lesson we still find difficult to learn.

## Jacob's Return to Bethel

A second tradition of a visit by Jacob to Bethel was placed in the narrative after the account of the rape of Dinah. God directed Jacob to leave Shechem and go to Bethel, where God had previously appeared to Jacob (35:1; see 28:10–17). Jacob first had his sons purify themselves, which included giving up all the idols and jewelry that they had (presumably things they had taken from the Shechemites), which Jacob then buried at "the oak that was near Shechem" (35:2–4). Was this oak among the oaks mentioned in connection to Abraham's first visit to Shechem (12:6)? Was it the same oak where Joshua later concluded a covenant between God and the people (Josh. 24:26)? Was it the same oak that even later marked the place where Abimelech was proclaimed king (Judg. 9:6)? There is no way to be certain, but traditions often are preserved at such sanctuaries, and this story of Dinah may have such a connection.

Jacob's trek to Bethel was remembered as "uneventful." Jacob had feared reprisals for the massacre his sons had carried out, but "a terror from God fell upon the cities all around them," and no one pursued (35:5). Jacob constructed an altar and called the place El-bethel, "God of Bethel" (35:6–7, 15; but see also 28:18–19; 33:18–20). Bethel was the place God had first directly revealed himself to Jacob as Jacob was fleeing from Esau's anger (28:10–22). Bethel was remembered also as the place where Deborah, Rebekah's nurse, died and was buried (35:8). But on the basis of this passage, Bethel was remembered because God once again appeared to Jacob and blessed him, changing his name (again? see 32:28) to Israel and reiterating the promise first given to Abraham and Sarah (12:2–3; 17:1–8; 22:15–18), then to Isaac and Rebekah (26:3–5), and now to Jacob and his family (35:11–12). Jacob appropriately remembered the occasion; he erected a pillar of stone and "poured out a drink offering on it, and poured oil on it" (35:14).

## Names for God

In the story of Jacob at Bethel God is called both "El-bethel" ("God of Bethel"; 35:7) and "El Shaddai," which is translated as "God Almighty" (35:11; 49:25). *Bethel* in Hebrew means "house of God." The Hebrew term *Shaddai* may indicate "mountains" or "female breasts." We do not know with certainty, so traditionally "Almighty" has been used in translations. It is not the primary term used in reference to God in Genesis, however.

There are a number of other names for God, of which just a few will be considered. "El Olam" was associated by tradition with a tamarisk tree planted by Abraham at Beer-sheba (21:33). The NRSV translates "El Olam" as "Everlasting God." The name "El-roi" ("God of seeing" or "God who sees") was used by Hagar after she was encountered by God (16:13). God was also likened to a "shield" (15:1), a "judge" (18:25), a "Mighty One," (49:24), a "shepherd" (49:24), and "the Rock of Israel" (49:24). The "Fear of Isaac" was also a phrase used in reference to God (31:42).

The basic term for "god" or "deity" in Hebrew and related Semitic languages was *el*. It was used by the Canaanites and other Mesopotamians to refer to the primary god, who was understood as the "father" of all the deities. That is the term that was used in conjunction with the various names already noted. The plural was *elohim*, which can simply mean "gods," but in Genesis and in much of the Bible "Elohim" was used in reference to the God of Israel. It has been interpreted as a "plural of majesty," thus meaning "Godliest God" or "Highest God" or something like that. "Elohim" was the name of the Creator in Genesis 1.

"YHWH" is another name for God that was used repeatedly in Genesis. For example, it is name of God in Genesis 2–3. As mentioned in chapter 1, this name is a personal name, and in Hebrew tradition remains unpronounceable. Modern scholars think that "Yahweh" is the most probable pronunciation. The NRSV has chosen to render YHWH as "Lord," and other translations sometimes use "Jehovah" for YHWH. According to biblical tradition YHWH was not revealed to humans until Moses' experience at the burning bush (Exod. 3:13–15). In Genesis, however, where stories much older than the time of Moses are recounted, both Elohim (God) and YHWH (Lord) are frequently found.

What are we to make of this profusion of ways to refer to God? Some scholars suggest that the various names, such as "El Olam" and "El-bethel," signal various local traditions that were taken over by the Israelites and slowly, over time, woven into the national story. Other scholars see only the result of a rich literary style that used a wide catalog of terminology to speak of the divine. Certainly there is ample evidence that numerous traditions have been brought together to fashion the book we now call Genesis. At the very least, what this rich variety should suggest to us is that there are numerous ways to refer to and talk about God. No one way is the only way; no one name alone is sufficient.

## Two More Notes

These "loose ends" stories we have been considering include two more of special note: the deaths of two important figures. The first has to do with the death of Rachel. She was pregnant when Jacob and his clan left Bethel and, on the way, went into hard labor (35:16). She was told by the midwife that she had a second son (35:17), but unfortunately Rachel began to fade during the birthing. So in her last breath, and according to the custom for mothers, she named her infant "Ben-oni" ("Son of my sorrow"). Jacob, however, perhaps because he misheard Rachel or for some other undisclosed reason, called the baby boy "Benjamin" ("Son of the south"). He then buried Rachel on the road outside Ephrath, later known as Bethlehem, and marked her tomb with a pillar (35:18–20). There is still a shrine that tradition marks as the place, just outside present-day Bethlehem. Modern Israelis and Palestinians have often clashed there, disputing the right of the one or the other's access, a fact that makes Rachel's name Ben-oni, Son of my sorrow, ironically fitting.

The second death to be noted is that of Isaac. Isaac had moved to Mamre or Hebron where Abraham and Sarah were buried (35:27; see 25:10). As had his father, Isaac was reported to have had an extraordinarily long life, one hundred eighty years according to the text (35:28). While Rachel had died an untimely death while still a relatively young woman, Isaac died "old and full of days" (35:29). What's more, his once-feuding sons, Jacob and Esau, came together peaceably to bury their father (35:29).

## Conclusion

This chapter has considered a number of stories loosely held together by their common reference to Jacob and his family. They reflect the widely diverse collection of traditions that the writer or writers of Genesis had at their disposal as they sought to sketch the early generations of the people of Israel. Some of the stories seem to contradict other portions of the account, but all were considered important and instructive. Thus we still listen to them and use them to shed light on our own proclivities and priorities. They provide a bright (though at times perhaps somewhat confusing) light.

# Chapter Seven

# The Providence of God

*A Study of Genesis 37:1–50:26*

## Introduction

The concluding chapters of Genesis (37–50) constitute what some scholars describe as a "novella" or "short story." There is a high degree of unity in the literary style and in the development of the story. There are a few passages, such as the engaging account about Judah and Tamar (38:1–30) and the revealing "last words of Jacob" (49:1–28), that break the narrative and may, in fact, be later additions to the text. Overall, however, these concluding chapters of Genesis, centering on Joseph, are developed in a dramatically impressive manner that carries the reader/hearer right along from beginning to end. We will not, however, attempt to consider the whole narrative. Nonetheless, the passages that will be examined will hopefully serve to provide a sufficient glimpse into the method and intention of the whole.

The Joseph story serves to connect the preceding Jacob stories or episodes with what follows in the book of Exodus. The account begins with the statement "Jacob settled in the land where his father had lived as an alien, the land of Canaan. This is the story of the family of Jacob" (37:1–2). The Joseph story relates how the fractured, competitive family of Jacob migrated from Canaan to Egypt, was able to prosper there, and finally became much more unified because of the trials they underwent. As readers we are prepared to understand how things could radically change so that Exodus, the next book of the Bible, can begin its account by describing Israel's situation as desperate (Exod. 1:1–8).

Stories of individuals that have been the focus in Genesis so far finally become the story of a family. The promise of land that was given to Abraham, Isaac, and Jacob as individuals is in the end bestowed by Joseph on the family, now the Israelites (50:24). From that point onward, the biblical narrative is about the people of God, Israel, and how they do or do not live into the divine intention that God has set before them.

## Joseph and His Dreams

The Joseph narrative begins when Joseph was seventeen, living in Canaan with his family. One of his duties was assisting his half brothers, the sons of Bilhah and Zilpah, shepherd the flocks. As in previous stories, we find the family to be highly conflicted. Because Jacob "loved Joseph more than any other of his children, because he was the son of his old age," he showed his favoritism by making a "long robe with sleeves" for Joseph alone (37:3). Joseph's siblings "hated" Joseph for two reasons: first, he was a tattletale ("brought a bad report") on his half brothers; second, he was clearly the favorite of their father, as Joseph's robe displayed to the world (37:2–3).

Two comments are in order before we continue. First, Joseph was indeed born after ten of the other brothers (30:22–24), but he was not the youngest of Jacob's children. Benjamin was truly the son of Jacob's "old age" (35:17–19), and later in the story Benjamin will be deemed most important to his father. Second, the garment Jacob gave to Joseph has come to be known popularly as the "coat of many colors" and has been the subject of song and art. From evidence gained in archaeological and linguistic research, however, we now know that the previous translation as "coat of many colors" is inaccurate. The NRSV more correctly rendered the Hebrew in question as "a long robe with sleeves" (37:3). The garment mentioned seems related to clothing worn by persons of authority in Egypt. For Jacob to give Joseph such a garment no doubt galled Joseph's brothers and increased their resentment of him.

In this climate of distrust Joseph reported two dreams to his brothers and father. Remember, as noted in chapter 5, dreams in antiquity were often considered a trustworthy medium for the revelation of divine purpose. Joseph's first dream was of a sheaf in the field, representing Joseph, receiving obeisance from other sheaves, representing his brothers (37:6–7). Joseph's brothers understood his dream to suggest that he was to rule over them, so they hated him all the more (37:5, 8).

The second dream was similar. He dreamed that "'the sun, the moon, and eleven stars were bowing down to [him]'" (37:9). When his father heard the dream, he reacted quite negatively. Were Jacob and the whole family to bow down to Joseph (37:10)? The tone of Jacob's question to his son signaled his understanding: No way! The dream disturbed Joseph's father and further fueled the jealousy of his brothers (37:11).

As a result of Joseph's dreams and the other aggravating circumstances of his presence among them, his brothers decided to get rid of Joseph. Jacob sent Joseph to check on his brothers who were shepherding near Shechem and bring back a report about their work (37:12–14). Joseph found his brothers at Dothan (37:17). When the brothers saw him coming from afar, they hatched a plot against him. They intended to kill him, throw his body in a pit, and then tell their father that a wild animal had devoured him (37:18–20). Reuben objected to killing Joseph, so the plan was altered to throwing him in a pit and leaving him to die of thirst. So they grabbed Joseph, tore off his long-sleeved robe, and threw him in a pit (37:22–24).

As it turned out, Joseph did not die of thirst. Both Judah and Reuben had second thoughts. Judah convinced his brothers to pull Joseph out of the pit and sell him to some Ishmaelite traders who were on their way to Egypt (37:25–27). Before they could do so, however, some Midianites came along, and "they drew Joseph up, lifting him out of the pit," and sold him as a slave to the Ishmaelites (37:28). Who "they" were that sold Joseph is ambiguous, however, in the Hebrew text. It could have been the brothers, and some translations make that choice. It seems more likely, however, that it was either the Midianites (37:36) or the Ishmaelites who later sold Joseph to an Egyptian official named Potiphar (39:1). At some point in time the Midianites and the Ishmaelites came to be viewed as one people (Judg. 8:22, 24).

Reuben went back to rescue Joseph, but Joseph was gone. When he reported this to his brothers, they took Joseph's robe, dipped it in the blood of a slaughtered goat, and took it to Jacob (37:29–32). When Jacob recognized the robe, he assumed that Joseph had been killed by a wild animal and went into inconsolable mourning for his lost son (37:33–35).

Because of his dreams—actually because of favoritism and sibling rivalry—Joseph ended up a slave in Egypt. This was certainly a disaster from Joseph's point of view, but as we will learn, God in God's providence was able to bring good out of or despite the human malice that brought this misfortune to pass.

## Joseph as a Dream Interpreter

As Joseph's story progesses, "bad" seems to have gone to "worse." The wife of the Egyptian Potiphar who had bought Joseph as a slave tried, with no success, to seduce Joseph (39:7–12), and when he refused her advances, she accused him of trying to rape her (39:13–18). As a result, Potiphar had him put into prison (39:19–20). But the narrator reassures the readers/hearers by reporting that "the LORD was with Joseph and showed him steadfast love" by bringing him into the favor of the chief jailer (39:21). Joseph was an imprisoned slave, but he was given a measure of privilege. The jailer put Joseph in charge of all the other prisoners, trusting Joseph completely (39:22–23).

While Joseph was serving as overseer of the jail, an unusual circumstance arose. He was put in charge of two of Pharaoh's former personal servants: the chief cupbearer and the chief baker who had offended Pharaoh and been imprisoned (40:1–4). "Pharaoh" is actually a title, not a name; it literally meant "big house" and was used to refer to the king somewhat like we use the term "White House" as a reference to the president. We do not know which pharaoh this was, but, while it would be interesting to know, it is not critical for the story.

One night each of Pharaoh's imprisoned servants had a troubling dream. When Joseph met them in the morning, he asked why they seemed so depressed. They confided that it was because they had no one to interpret the meaning of their dreams (40:5–8). Joseph volunteered to hear the dreams, but he hedged his bets, so to speak, by commenting, "'Do not interpretations belong to God?'" (40:8).

The chief cupbearer shared his dream first, and Joseph interpreted it as a positive sign that Pharaoh would soon restore the cupbearer to his position in court (40:9–13). Joseph then asked the cupbearer to remember him when he was released to help get Joseph out of prison (40:14–15). When the chief baker heard Joseph's interpretation of the cupbearer's dream, he was encouraged and disclosed his dream as well. Unfortunately, Joseph understood the baker's dream to be an announcement of his impending execution (40:16–19). Within three days, Pharaoh restored the cupbearer to his former position and executed the baker (40:20–22)! Was Joseph's situation remedied? No, for "the chief cupbearer did not remember Joseph, but forgot him" (40:23).

## Joseph's Rise to Power

This detailed account of Joseph and the dreams is masterfully told. It provides the background to understand the pivotal event toward which the narrator was moving. Two years later, Pharaoh had two dreams, and no one was able to interpret them (41:1–8), so Pharaoh was troubled. Then the cupbearer remembered the young Hebrew slave who had rightly interpreted his dream (41:9–13). He told Pharaoh of him, and Joseph was brought before Pharaoh (41:14).

Pharaoh told Joseph his dreams and asked him to interpret them. Joseph disavowed any special power but assured Pharaoh, "'God will give Pharaoh a favorable answer'" (41:16). After Joseph heard the dreams, he explained to Pharaoh that the dreams meant that there were going to be seven good years when there would be great prosperity, followed by seven lean years that would be severely hard (41:17–31). Because Pharaoh had received two dreams that meant essentially the same thing, Joseph considered it a sign that it was "fixed by God" and would soon happen (41:32). Thus Joseph encouraged Pharaoh to appoint trustworthy people to arrange to have food stored during the good years so that there could be enough for all during the bad years (41:33–36).

Guess what? Surprise, surprise; Joseph was made the one, the "man"! Because of his great wisdom Joseph was given command over all Pharaoh's land (41:37–41) and assigned all the privileges and powers that went with being Pharaoh's right-hand man (41:42–44). He was given an Egyptian name, an Egyptian wife, and total authority (41:45). At the age of thirty, Joseph's situation had dramatically improved (41:46). During the next years he carried out the storage of food as he had suggested (41:47–49), and Asenath, his wife, bore him two sons, Manasseh and Ephraim (41:50–52).

When the years of famine came, Joseph was ready. All Egypt came to him to buy grain—indeed, all the world came to Joseph in Egypt (41:53–57). As we will see later, Joseph was still a slave, but the disliked "brat" who had pushed his brothers to the verge of murder had risen to a place where he would be able to determine the life or death of many, including his whole family.

Several comments need to be made at this point. While there is no way to prove the historicity of this account, the Egyptian setting is convincingly described. We know from extrabiblical records and from archaeological work that the names that are mentioned, for instance, are Egyptian. The form of government is also correctly reflected, and periods of famine and plenty in Egypt and in the wider region can be documented. Semitic groups traveled back and forth into Egypt and out of it seeking good pastures and buying food when famine came to the region. An active slave trade between Mesopotamia and Egypt, some of which passed through the land of Canaan, existed. And, perhaps most surprising, there are records that tell of slaves who were placed in positions of great authority by their masters and who carried out their responsibilities quite well. So while the account can't be shown to be "historically true," it is certainly believable.

From the narrator's point of view, this whole sequence of events was the result of the mysterious hand of God. The least of the brothers had become the foremost, just as God had revealed to them would happen so many years earlier (37:1–11). Providentially, God was going to bring this struggling, sometimes quarreling and obnoxious family into a new situation. Jacob, the man, was in fact on the verge of becoming Israel, the people.

## Joseph Is Reunited with His Brothers

As already suggested, the years of famine did not spare Jacob's family. Canaan was hard hit. Jacob heard that there was grain that could be purchased in Egypt, so he sent ten of his sons, Joseph's brothers, to get some (42:1–3). His youngest son, Benjamin, Joseph's younger and only full brother, stayed with Jacob in Canaan, lest something bad should happen to him (42:4–5).

When Joseph's brothers arrived, Joseph recognized them, but they did not recognize him (42:8). There follows a detailed account of how Joseph brought distress and uncertainty to his brothers, imprisoning them as spies (42:6–17) and holding Simeon as a "hostage" who would be released only if they brought their youngest brother, Benjamin, back from Canaan as proof of their integrity (42:18–24). The brothers interpreted this as the penalty for what they had done to Joseph many years before (42:21–22).

The story becomes all the more involved. Joseph's brothers went back to their father and finally convinced him to allow them to take Benjamin with them when they returned for more food (42:26–43:10). When they returned, they brought a gift for the man in charge—we know it is Joseph, but they did not—and they brought double an amount of money that had been given to them mistakenly (they believed) on their previous trip. And they brought Benjamin (43:11–15).

The narrator builds more and more tension as the story continues. The brothers were pushed to their limit by Joseph, not knowing what he was up to or what would befall them (43:16–34). Benjamin was retained (by a ruse that Joseph arranged), and the brothers, particularly Judah, pled for his release (44:1–34). The details are engaging, but the question arises, "Wasn't Joseph being somewhat vindictive?" He put his brothers through a great deal of agony and stress, and for what? He felt anguish himself at several points, and he could have resolved the situation immediately if he had wanted. Why didn't he? The narrator would perhaps say, "For the sake of a great story."

Whether we agree that literary license is sufficient justification for all the story's details, it is important to note how much we learn about the way the family has matured. Judah, especially, is shown to be much more sensitive and caring about his brother and their father than when he was younger (43:8–10; 44:18–34). (From the tribe of Judah David, son of Jesse, would eventually emerge to be king of Judah [2 Sam. 2:1–4].) The other brothers also reflect a sense of moral culpability and responsibility at several points in ways hard to imagine of them in their earlier years (42:21–22, 26–28; 43:18–22; 44:7–9). Joseph also moves beyond what may at first have been a degree of spitefulness to a genuine affection for his brothers. And yes, it is a very good story.

The climax is reached when Joseph finally chose to reveal his identity to his brothers. The brothers were gathered before Joseph, and, as the text puts it, "Joseph could no longer control himself before all those who stood by him" (45:1). He sent everyone out of the room but his brothers. Then he wept loudly and told his brothers who he was (45:2–3). Next comes the whole point of this long story, at least as far as the narrator was concerned. Joseph said,

> I am your brother, Joseph, whom you sold into Egypt. And now do not be distressed, or angry with yourselves, because you sold me here; for God sent me before you to preserve life. . . . God sent me before you to preserve for you a remnant on earth, and to keep alive for you many survivors. So it was not you who sent me here, but God. (45:4–8)

Joseph instructed his brothers to hurry back to Jacob, assuring him that Joseph was alive. They were to bring Jacob and all the family to Egypt, where Pharaoh offered them ample supplies and fertile land on which to live (45:9–20).

This is a moving moment in Joseph's story. His capacity to reach out to the brothers who so deeply wronged him is amazing. His rationalization of what had happened to them all, however, is somewhat disturbing. If taken too far, any human misbehavior could be excused as long as there is a relatively "happy" ending. God may well be involved in the unfolding of events, but human responsibility is still expected. The interpretation of the whole event as "God's work" should not be taken as license for simply muddling along and hoping things will work out.

## Joseph Passes On the Promise

The famine that ate away at all Egypt and Canaan had continued for two years when Joseph sent his brothers to bring Jacob to Egypt. According to Joseph, there were five more lean years to come (45:6). Jacob's sons returned to their father and reported that Joseph was alive and in a position of prominence. They also informed Jacob of Joseph's invitation to come to Egypt (45:25–27). Jacob was overjoyed at the news (45:28). With his whole family he set out from Beer-sheba for Egypt (46:1, 5–27). In preparation for the journey Jacob offered sacrifices "to the God of his father Isaac" (46:1), who then appeared to him in a night vision (46:2) in which the promise of progeny that had been repeated regularly across the course of the longer story of Abraham and Isaac once again was pronounced (46:3). As before, when Jacob left the land promised to his forebears, God's presence and protection were assured (46:4).

Thanks to the generosity of Pharaoh, Jacob settled in Goshen (45:18; 46:28), which was situated northeast of the capitol in the Nile delta. According to the narrator the Egyptians did not like shepherding as an occupation (though there are no Egyptian documents to suggest this); thus Joseph arranged for them to be in Goshen, far removed from the capital, with rich pasturage available (46:33–34; 47:1–6). After Joseph's moving reunion with his father (46:28–30), Joseph arranged for Pharaoh to meet his father. Jacob blessed Pharaoh when he first met him and as he departed (47:7, 10), acts that made concrete God's promise that the nations who blessed Israel would in turn be blessed (12:3).

Jacob lived in Egypt seventeen years. Toward the end of Jacob's life, Joseph, with his sons Manasseh and Ephraim, borne by Joseph's Egyptian wife Asenath (48:1–2; see 41:45, 50–52), went to Jacob. (It should be noted that in later years the tribes of Ephraim and Manasseh occupied the hill country north of Jerusalem. These tribes, Joseph's "sons," were at the center of what came to be the kingdom of Israel, which rivaled the kingdom of Judah from 922 BCE to 722 BCE when Israel was destroyed by the Assyrians.) For the first time, so far as the story is concerned, Jacob told one of his sons, Joseph, about God's promise of progeny and land (48:4). Jacob explained how that promise was to be extended to Joseph, Joseph's sons, and Joseph's brothers (48:5–7). No longer would the promise rest with a single individual.

Jacob then blessed his two grandsons. In doing so, however, in a reversal we have become accustomed to in Genesis, Jacob crossed his hands and rested his right hand (with the greater blessing) on Ephraim, the younger grandson, and his left on the older, Manasseh (48:14). Joseph protested, but Jacob insisted that Ephraim was to be the greater of the two (48:17–20). When Jacob died, he was given full Egyptian burial rites, including embalming, and then with great ceremony his body was taken to Hebron, as he had asked, and placed in the cave of Machpelah with his forebears (49:29–50:14).

The story is concluded, but not quite. Joseph's brothers became concerned that Joseph might still hold a grudge against them (50:15). It is at this point that we reach the final climax of story. Joseph responded to his brothers with this simple but profound (though somewhat problematic) statement: "'Do not be afraid! Am I in the place of God? Even though you intended to do harm to me, God intended it for good, in order to preserve a numerous people, as he is doing today'" (50:18–20). Thus the promise made to Abraham, to Isaac, and then to Jacob was passed by Joseph to the whole family. Joseph's body, too, would one day be returned to the land of Canaan, the land of promise, by the Israelites (50:24–25; see Exod. 13:19).

The book of Genesis concludes on a note of mystery. How can we know what God intends? Is anything that happens simply to be accepted as the "will of God"? Many have so interpreted Joseph's story. Trust in the working of God in the midst of all the good and bad of life must be carefully nuanced. Humankind is expected to act responsibly in cooperation with God. We are not to "accept" the injustices of our world as just the "will of God." At the same time, however, we can rest assured that God does care and is able to bring good out of the worst of situations.

## Conclusion

The Joseph story is well crafted and thought provoking. It is an exciting tale! There is enough "historically accurate" detail about life in Egypt to make it believable. The principal characters are presented in a way that helps us get in touch with them. Once again, we find real people with real problems struggling in a very real world in many ways like our own. That is the aim of all good literature!

*Part Two*

# LEADER'S GUIDE

## DONALD L. GRIGGS

# Guidelines for Bible Study Leaders

## The Bible from Scratch Series

This is one of a series of Bible study courses designed for people who want to study the Bible but who are reluctant to join a group of Bible study veterans. Many fear they will be embarrassed and will not be able to use the Bible and participate comfortably. This series, however, makes no assumptions about what someone should know regarding the Bible; thus it is identified as a course for beginners. Many who come to your class, however, will no doubt not be beginners with the Bible but will nevertheless desire to engage in a course that deals with the basics for Bible study.

## Goals of the Course

Even though this course on Genesis could be read and studied without one's being a member of a class, the greatest value of the study will be realized when the reader is engaged with others who are companions on the journey. As I prepared these session plans I had in mind the following five goals that I hoped participants would experience as a result of their study:

1. Participants will bring to their study a desire to enter more deeply into the world of the Bible and, in this study, the world of Genesis.

2. Class members will enjoy studying the Bible with others.

3. Participants will come to a greater understanding and appreciation of the origins, structure, and message of Genesis.

4. Prompted by what they read and think, class members will share their insights, questions, and affirmations with one another.

5. Participants will develop a discipline of reading and studying the Bible on a regular basis.

## Basic Teaching Principles

As I prepared these session plans, I tried to implement a number of basic principles for effective teaching and leading. The foundational principle is an attempt to involve everyone in the class in as many activities as possible at every session. That's a big goal! Though it is not possible to succeed with everyone, there are many opportunities for individuals to participate every week, and most will if they are encouraged to do so. You will see this principle present in all of the session plans that follow. I also had the following ten principles in mind as I designed this course:

1. The leader does not have to be an expert but serves best as companion and guide in the journey of the course.

2. The leader provides sufficient information but not so much that participants lose the joy of discovery.

3. Motivation for learning involves enjoying the process, completing tasks, and making choices.

4. Participants learn best when a variety of activities and resources are used that appeal to their different interests, needs, and learning styles.

5. Participants need to be invited to express their feelings, ideas, and beliefs in creative ways that are appropriate to them and to the subject matter.

6. Everyone needs opportunities to share what he or she under-stands and believes.

7. Open-ended questions invite interpretation, reflection, and application.

8. Persons are nurtured in faith when they share their faith sto-ries with one another.

9. All teaching and learning happens in planned and unplanned ways and is for the purpose of increasing biblical literacy and faithful discipleship.

10. The Bible becomes the living word of God when teach-ers and learners see their own faith stories expressed in Scripture.

## Room Arrangement

Arrange the room where you meet in such a way that participants are seated at tables so that class members have space for their Bibles, other materials, and their coffee cups. Tables also suggest that the class is going to work and not just sit and listen to a lecture. If members of the group do not know other members by name, they all need name tags. Set up a table with hot water and makings for coffee, tea, and hot chocolate just inside the entrance to the room so everyone can get a cup and then find a seat. If you have a small group, arrange the tables in a rectangle or square so that everyone can see all the other members of the group. With a small group, you will be able to be seated with them. On the other hand, if you have a large group, arrange the tables in a fan shape pointed toward the front so the participants can see the leader standing at a lectern or small table with whiteboard, newsprint easel, or bulletin board.

## Resources

On the first week, be sure to provide Bibles for those who do not bring one. Continue to provide Bibles for those activities when it is important for everyone to have the same translation and edition if you plan for them all to look at the same pages at the same time. However, continue to encourage everyone to bring his or her own Bible. In addition to the Bibles, borrow from the church library, the pastor's library, and your own library copies of Bible dictionaries, Genesis commentaries, and Bible atlases. A church library will not ordinarily have enough Bible source books for each person to have one, so for those sessions where members are responsible for searching for information about a passage, person, or event in Genesis, make photocopies of the appropriate articles from a Bible dictionary, encyclopedia, or atlas. For one-time use, for one class, such copying is not a violation of copyright law.

Be sure to provide paper and pencils for those who don't bring them. Almost all of the activity sheets to be used by the participants are at the end of the respective session plans for which they will be used, so each participant needs to have a copy of this course book. If some class members cannot afford to purchase a copy or prefer not to, arrange to have several copies available for them to borrow.

## Time

I planned each session to be an hour in length, so if you have less than an hour, you will have to make adjustments. It will be better to leave out an activity than to rush class members through all of the suggested activities, or perhaps it would be possible in your situation to schedule more than seven meetings. There is probably enough material here for eight to ten sessions. If you can arrange for additional sessions, you would truly be able to deal with everything carefully without hurrying.

If you and your group have not already studied one of the first two books in this Bible study series, *The Bible from Scratch: The Old Testament for Beginners* or *The Bible from Scratch: The New Testament for Beginners,* you may find it helpful to use session 1 from either of those courses as an introduction to this style of Bible study.

## Final Word

As you prepare to teach this course, it is essential that you read each chapter of the Participant's Guide as you consider your teaching strategy for each session of the course. You should assume that many, though not all, of the participants will have read the respective chapter before coming to class, and you should be as familiar with the material as they are. Exploring Genesis with fellow pilgrims on the journey of faith will be for them and for you a challenging, inspiring, growing, and satisfying experience. May God bless you with many discoveries and much joy on this journey. If you and the members of your Bible study group have found this course to be helpful, you may want to look for other Bible studies in the series.

Livermore, California
September 2009

# *Session One*

# Beginnings

*A Study of Genesis 1:1–2:25; 6:1–22; 9:1–17*

## BEFORE THE SESSION
### Focus of the Session

In this first session it will be important to get started "on the right foot" by welcoming everyone, helping participants get acquainted with one another, and introducing the course of study. The two main topics of this session are the two narratives of creation and the narrative of Noah and the flood.

### Advance Preparation

- Take the time to read the selected portions of Genesis for this session.

- If you are able to read through the whole book of Genesis, it will provide both background and perspective for understanding the selected portions.

- Read an introductory article or two about the book of Genesis in a study Bible, Bible dictionary, or Bible commentary.

- Read articles in a Bible dictionary that deal with "documentary hypothesis," "Pentateuch," and names for God, such as "*elohim*," "YHWH," or "*Yahweh*."

- Gather several Bible study tools to share with the participants: a single-volume Bible commentary, a Bible dictionary, and one or more study Bibles. These will be the same resources volunteers will use to prepare brief presentations for the next session.

- Prepare two large sheets of newsprint in order to record the answers of the small groups when they report their answers from the "Comparing Two Creation Narratives" activity.

- One suggested activity is to bring several children's storybooks of the Noah-and-the-flood narrative to class. If you don't have any in your personal library, you certainly can find one in the church school or church library, or perhaps a friend with children will have a book or two that you can borrow. Of course, there is always the city library.

- Provide a few extra Bibles for those who forget to bring one.

- Do a little research to find sources and prices of study Bibles, preferably the NRSV, which is the translation on which this study is based. This research will enable you to respond to persons who inquire about a study Bible after you have mentioned their value. (You will find a list of recommended study Bibles in the appendix.)

## Physical Arrangements

Reread the section of the "Guidelines for Bible Study Leaders" that offers suggestions regarding room arrangement, resources and materials, and refreshments. You should have everything ready for the first session. You will want to get off to a good start, especially for those who are new to Bible study.

## Teaching Alternatives

The session plan that follows assumes a minimum of an hour for the study session. If you have less than an hour, then you will need to make some adjustments in the plan, such as (1) extending the session to two sessions, (2) skipping the building-community activity if the members of the group already know each other fairly well, or (3) eliminating another activity.

## DURING THE SESSION
## Welcoming the Participants

Arrive at class early enough to set up the refreshments and have everything ready before the first persons arrive. Ask the participants to sign in and make name tags for themselves. Greet each one by name with a warm welcome. As the group gathers, be sure to remind them of the five goals on page 68. Check to see which participants need to borrow a Bible, and give them one. Also, encourage them to bring a Bible next week. If any of the participants do not already have a copy of this course book, you should give them one so they will have access to any of the references you will make to it during the session and especially to the worksheets.

## Introducing the Course

After all have arrived and you have welcomed the participants, share with the group an overview of what to expect in this course. Here are some points to emphasize:

- This first session will introduce the class to Genesis and guide them to focus on the creation and Noah narratives.

- The remaining six sessions will focus on selected narratives in Genesis in chronological order. The narratives of the fifty chapters of Genesis are too many to deal with in a short course. However, the narratives that are chosen will provide a helpful overview of the whole book.

- The session plans will not necessarily repeat what is in the Participant's Guide but will be based on that material and the related portions of Genesis.

- Participants are expected to read the relevant chapter in the Participant's Guide in preparation for each session.

- They should bring a Bible to class, preferably a study Bible if they have one.

- Their understanding and appreciation of Genesis will be enhanced greatly if they read the selected passages in preparation for each session.

- There will be some presentation by the leader in each session, but most of the time the leader will be guiding the participants through a series of activities designed to engage participants with the key Scriptures and main ideas of that session.

- There are no "dumb questions." All questions are appropriate. Encourage the participants to ask questions of the leader and the group.

- Everyone's insights, ideas, and affirmations will be received and respected. It is important to feel free to express what is in one's mind and heart.

Begin the journey through Genesis with a brief litany prayer based on Psalm 148.

## Opening Prayer

Introduce this activity by stating that in each session there will be an opening prayer that will be prompted by words from Scripture. This session's opening prayer is in the form of a litany based on Psalm 148. It is not necessary for the participants to turn to Psalm 148 since you will lead them in the following steps:

- Introduce Psalm 148 as a hymn of praise to God the Creator. This psalm is quite appropriate since featured passages in this session are Genesis 1 and 2, the creation narratives.

- The phrase "Praise the Lord" appears frequently in this psalm.

- Tell the group that every time you give them a signal with a hand gesture they are to say in unison, "Praise the Lord."

- Read a verse or part of a verse at a time. Each time the word "Praise" or the phrase "Praise the Lord" appears, signal the group to respond.

- You can signal for a few additional responses as you read. For instance, in verses 8 to 12 the phrase doesn't appear, but adding a few "Praise the Lords" would enhance the litany.

- When you get to the end of the psalm, invite participants to suggest some things from their lives for which they praise the Lord. After each shares something, prompt the group to continue the litany response.

## Building Community among the Participants

In this first session take time for participants to introduce themselves so that they can begin getting acquainted with other members of the group. Invite them to introduce themselves by stating three things: their name, a memory of a Sunday school or adult class attended in the past, and a favorite story in the Bible or in Genesis if they remember any of those narratives. Be sure to introduce yourself in this activity, perhaps first in order to model what you have in mind. After all have been introduced, affirm what has been shared and indicate that you have heard some wonderful memories and favorite Bible stories and that they are a great foundation on which to build this study of the book of Genesis.

## Introducing Genesis

Spend a few minutes making a brief introduction to the book of Genesis. Consider including the following key points in your presentation:

- Explain the origin of the book's title.

- Mention that Genesis is divided into two major sections: chapters 1–11, which deal with the beginnings or prehistory; and chapters 12–50, which deal with Abraham and his descendants.

- You could invite the group to flip through the pages of Genesis to see what the major narratives are in both sections.

- Review quickly how Genesis is a composite of several traditions gathered in this one book over a period of several centuries. Make reference to the Participant's Guide, pages 7–9.

- Speak about the two names for God that appear most frequently in Genesis: the Hebrew word *elohim,* which is rendered as God in Genesis; and YHWH, which is rendered as LORD, the proper name of God revealed to Moses at the time of his encounter with the Almighty when a bush was burning but not being consumed.

- If you feel that you have sufficient time and think the group will not be sidetracked, and if you are comfortable with the subject, you could spend a few minutes commenting on the theory of the documentary hypothesis.

## Comparing Two Creation Narratives

In the Participant's Guide (pp. 8–11) we are introduced to two different accounts of how God created the earth and all living creatures. One is identified as the "earliest account" (2:4b–25), and the other, as "the later account" (1:1–2:4a). Make reference to what was shared in the previous presentation regarding several different sources or traditions and explain that in this activity you are going to compare the two different creation narratives.

- Direct the class members to the worksheet on page 80 of the Leader's Guide.

- Divide the participants into two smaller groups. One group is to answer the questions based on Genesis 1:1–2:4a while the second group answers the questions for 2:4b–25. (You may need to explain about the use of a and b in the verse citations.)

- If your group has more than twelve participants, you could divide them differently by having them form small groups of five or six and then assign two or more groups one narrative and the remaining groups the second narrative.

- They should be able to complete their task in about ten minutes.

- Join together as a whole class. Invite the participants to share answers to the eight questions for both creation accounts.

- Record answers one question at a time on a grid you have prepared on newsprint or a whiteboard.

- When all the answers have been recorded, spend a few minutes reflecting on what has been presented. Guide the reflection with a question or two. Here are some examples:

> What are some observations or insights you have when you consider the differences between these two accounts of creation?
>
> What do you make of the humans having "dominion" over the creatures? What are the differences between having dominion over and exploiting the creatures?
>
> What do you see as the central message of both accounts?
>
> What do these first two chapters suggest to you about what you might expect to discover when you consider the Bible as a whole?

## Exploring the Noah Narrative

It would be helpful for you as leader to review notes in a Bible commentary or study Bible before leading this part of the session. You will want to sort out the facts of the narrative, have in mind the story's key truths, and determine how to avoid the pitfall of getting sidetracked by questions regarding the historicity of the events in Genesis 6 to 8. The story of Noah and the flood is perhaps one of the most familiar and the most misunderstood of any of the biblical narratives. Although the focus on all the animals is what makes the Noah story popular among children, it is also a story that can be confusing to children. The following suggestions will help you explore the Noah narrative with your class:

- Try to find one or more children's storybooks of the Noah-and-the-flood story to bring to class. Take the time to read one of the stories to the class, then open the discussion with several questions:

> Why do you think there are so many children's books based on the story of Noah and the flood?
>
> How does this story compare with the biblical narrative?
>
> What is the main point of the children's story?
>
> Why might the Noah story not be a good one to share with children?

- Take time to review the outline of the narrative in Genesis 6 to 8. As you review the story call attention to some of the discrepancies in the narrative; the symbolic number of days, forty and seven; the symbolism of the raven and the dove; and the significance of the concept of covenant.

- In the Participant's Guide, March writes, "To get caught up in questions of the historicity of the account in Genesis is to risk missing the point" (p. 13). Explore with the class what they think he means by that statement.

- March also proposes three key points to gain from the narrative (p. 14). Read aloud those three points and then spend a few minutes discussing several questions:

> What do these three points suggest to you regarding the relationship between God and human beings?
>
> Are there any other points that you would like to add to these three?
>
> We have looked at two creation narratives and a flood narrative as the beginning of the book of Genesis. What do these narratives communicate to you regarding God, the natural world, and human beings?

## Closing

There are several possibilities for closing the session. If you are running short of time, you will need to decide which of the following you will be able to do in the time available.

Sing together "He's Got the Whole World in His Hands." You could invite the class members to suggest words for some of the verses.

- Read together "Psalm 8: A Choral Reading" found on page 81. Ask for two volunteers to read the two solo verses and then proceed with the reading.

- Conclude with a brief prayer of praise and thanksgiving to God for God's creative power and steadfast love.

## AFTER THE SESSION

In next week's session there is an opportunity for one or two class members to make brief presentations based on some reading and research they will do ahead of time on the concept of covenant. Ask if there is anyone who is willing to read articles in one or two Bible dictionaries or comments in one or two Bible commentaries on Genesis 17. If you have a couple of volunteers then you will need to provide them with the resources and directions for the assignment.

Encourage the participants to read chapter 2 of the Participant's Guide, "A Promise Is a Promise," and the corresponding portions of Genesis, 12:1–20; 17:1–27; and 22:1–19.

| Comparing Two Creation Narratives | | |
|---|---|---|
| Genesis 1:1–2:4a | Questions to Answer | Genesis 2:4b–25 |
| 1. | Where is the "place" of creation? | 1. |
| 2. | What is the "duration" of creation? How long did it take? | 2. |
| 3. | By what "means" does God do the creating? | 3. |
| 4. | What is the sequence in which God does the creating? | 4. |
| 5. | When in the sequence is the male being created? Of what "substance"? | 5. |
| 6. | When in the sequence is the female being created? Of what "substance"? | 6. |
| 7. | What is the relationship between male and female? | 7. |
| 8. | What is the relationship between God and the human beings? | 8. |

## Psalm 8: A Choral Reading

All:
*O LORD, our Sovereign,
how majestic is your name in all the earth!*

Men:
You have set your glory above the heavens.

Women:
Out of the mouths of babes and infants
you have founded a bulwark because of your foes,
to silence the enemy and the avenger.

Solo 1:
When I look at your heavens, the work of your fingers,
the moon and the stars that you have established;

Solo 2:
what are human beings that you are mindful of them,
mortals that you care for them?

All:
*Yet you have made them a little lower than God,
and crowned them with glory and honor.*

Men:
You have given them dominion over the works of your hands;
you have put all things under their feet,

Women:
all sheep and oxen,
and also the beasts of the field,

Men:
the birds of the air, and the fish of the sea,
whatever passes along the paths of the seas.

All:
*O LORD, our Sovereign,
how majestic is your name in all the earth!*

## Session Two

# A Promise Is a Promise

*A Study of Genesis 12:1–20; 17:1–27; 22:1–19*

### BEFORE THE SESSION
#### Focus of the Session

The focus of this session will be on three chapters of Genesis with an emphasis on faithful obedience to God and God's covenant relationship with Abraham and his descendants. We will consider the importance of names and the changing of names in the Bible, and we will deal with the difficult-to-understand narrative of Abraham's sacrifice of his son Isaac.

#### Advance Preparation

- Take the time to read the selected portions of Genesis for this session: 12:1–20; 17:1–27; 22:1–19.

- Read the comments and notes of the selected Genesis passages in a study Bible or commentary.

- Read articles in a Bible dictionary that deal with "covenant."

- Locate a set of maps of Bible lands or a Bible atlas where you will be able to show the sites mentioned in the "Getting Our Geographical Bearings" activity. The two maps on pages 123 and 124 will also be helpful.

- Provide a few extra Bibles for those who forget to bring one.

## Teaching Alternatives

The session plan that follows assumes a minimum of an hour for the study. If you have less than an hour, then you could extend the session to two sessions, or you could eliminate the "Reviewing Session One" activity.

## DURING THE SESSION
## Welcoming the Participants

Arrive at class early enough to set up the refreshments and to have everything ready before the first persons arrive. Ask the participants to sign in and make name tags for themselves, which is especially important if participants do not know one another's names. Greet each one by name with a warm welcome, and be sure to notice newcomers who were not present at the first session. Welcome them, give them a copy of the course book and a Bible if they did not bring one, and assure them that they will catch on quickly with the content and process. Check to see who needs to borrow a Bible, and give them one and encourage them to bring a Bible next week.

## Opening Prayer

Begin this class session with a brief prayer in which you invite the participants to contribute to the prayer in a process as follows:

- Introduce the prayer by stating that in this session they will be exploring several passages in Genesis that are focused on Abraham, who is shown as a man who had faith in God.

- Invite the participants to suggest situations in the world, community, church, or their own lives where we need to have faith in God.

- After each suggestion is expressed, invite the group to respond in unison, "Gracious God, may we have sufficient faith to trust you." (It will be helpful to write this response on a sheet of newsprint so that everyone can see the words.)

## Reviewing Session One

Spend a few minutes reviewing the previous session for the sake of those who were not present and to take advantage of the reading everyone else did. Be sure not to get sidetracked in this activity because there is a lot to cover in this session. Conduct the review by doing the following:

- Start by asking, "What were the three key narratives we focused on last session?" (The answer should include the two different creation narratives and the narrative of Noah and the flood).

- Ask a second question: "What are the main points you remember from session 1?"

- Conclude by stating that this session and the five that follow will focus on selective, key passages that will provide an overview of the faith and foibles of Abraham and his kin: Isaac, Esau, Jacob, and Joseph.

## Getting Our Geographical Bearings

Before examining the Abraham narratives, it would be helpful to spend a few minutes providing a geographical orientation. Somewhere among your church's Christian education resources you should be able to find a set of Bible maps. If not, perhaps the church library or pastor's library will have an atlas that includes a map of the Near East at the time of Abraham and the patriarchs. You want the participants to see where the following sites mentioned in Genesis 11 and 12 are located: Ur, Haran, Canaan, Shechem, Bethel, Negeb, and Egypt. You should also be able to show the route between Ur, Haran, Canaan, and Egypt, an area known as the Fertile Crescent. It will be helpful for the class members to see the relative distances between the sites. The maps on pages 123 and 124 will also be helpful.

## Reflecting on Call, Journey, and Deceit

Having journeyed from Ur, the family of Terah, including his son and daughter-in-law, Abram and Sarai, settled in Haran. While living in Haran, Abram was called by God to go to a new land. The journey took Abram through Canaan to the Negeb and eventually to Egypt. While in Egypt there was the deceit prompted by Abram's claiming Sarai to be his sister instead of his wife. Genesis 12 presents us with contrasting views of Abram as a man of faithful obedience as well as one who is fearful, without trust in God.

After reviewing the narrative of Genesis 12, spend a few minutes in discussion guided by questions such as the following:

- How would you characterize the relationship between Abram and God?

- Considering that these narratives were composed at a later time, when the people were well settled in Canaan at the time of the monarchy, what do you see as the purpose and meaning of this narrative of Abram and Sarai?

- Why do you suppose Abram was so trusting when responding to the Lord's call to leave Haran and later so untrusting when his family went to Egypt to find food?

- What are some examples of times when you have been trusting and untrusting of God?

## Exploring the Concept of Covenant

We were introduced to the concept of "covenant" in Genesis 9 and the narratives associated with Noah. In Genesis 17 the concept of covenant is prominent again with the word appearing ten times. In the Participant's Guide, pages 18–20, "Living in Covenant," the author describes how the covenant God made with Abraham is different from the covenant made with Moses. It will be important to help the participants understand the differences between the two types of covenants and to identify the significance of the covenant relationship established by God with Abraham. In this part of the session you will take either of the following two approaches:

*First Approach:* If last week you asked for volunteers to do a little research on the concept of covenant, they could make their brief presentations at this time.

*Second Approach:* If no participants volunteered, then you should make the brief presentation about covenant.

After the presentation by group members or by you, continue with a brief discussion on the significance of this concept to understanding the relationship between God and Abraham and his descendants. The discussion could be guided by the questions that follow or ones you have prepared.

- What are some other narratives in the Bible where the concept of covenant is a central feature in the narrative?

- What do you see as the nature or significance of God's covenant with Abraham?

- To what extent is the understanding of covenant relevant to a Christian's faith relationship with God today?

- What are some ways our covenant relationship with God is symbolized?

## Considering the Importance of Names

In Genesis 17:5 and 17:15, Abram and Sarai's names are changed by God to Abraham and Sarah. In Hebrew, the name Abraham means "father of a multitude" and Sarah means "princess," suggesting she will be the mother of kings. Names are very important in the Old Testament, including the name of God, which was revealed to Moses in his encounter with God at the burning bush. Spend a few minutes focusing on the importance of names.

- Introduce the topic by stating that in the Old Testament names are very important. A person's name has meaning that tells you something about the person.

- Look at Genesis 17:5 and 17:15 where Abram's and Sarai's names are changed.

- Ask the participants if they can think of other examples in the Bible where names of persons were changed. (Some examples include Jacob to Israel, Simon to Peter, and Saul to Paul.)

- Invite the class members to share any stories that are associated with their names. If there are any married women who have taken their husband's last name as their own, ask them to share what it was like to have a new name. Also, ask if parents have any brief stories to share regarding their experience of naming their children.

- Conclude with the question "How would you summarize the importance of naming and names in the Bible compared to how we think of names and naming today?"

## Reflecting on Abraham's Sacrifice of Isaac

One of the most difficult narratives to understand in Genesis, if not the whole Bible, is the account in Genesis 22 of Abraham's being directed by God to prepare to offer his son Isaac as a sacrifice. In this narrative we are confronted with a moral dilemma. On the one hand, human sacrifice is condemned in that God provides an animal to be the sacrifice instead of Isaac while, on the other hand, Abraham is commended for his absolute obedience to God in that he was willing to sacrifice his son. As you lead your class through Genesis 22 there are several things you might consider doing:

- Without looking directly at Genesis 22, lead the group through a re-creation of the narrative of Abraham's sacrifice of Isaac based on what they remember of the story. You may have to fill in some of the gaps where memory is not clear.

- In Gen. 22:1, in response to God's addressing him by name, Abraham responds, "Here I am." The same response appears again at critical moments in verses 7 and 11. Call attention to the occasions where Abraham is addressed by God, by his son, and by God again. Reflect on these responses briefly with the question "What do you think the writer of Genesis was seeking to communicate about the character of Abraham through the repetition of this response?" You might also refer to Moses (Exod. 3:4) and Samuel (1 Sam. 3:4, 6, 8), who had identical responses to God's calling them. There is also the favorite hymn of many, "Here I Am, Lord."

- Spend some time reflecting on the narrative with the following questions or ones that you will prepare:

    What is the most difficult aspect of this narrative to understand? Why?

How might the author of this portion of Genesis be presenting this story in order to condemn the ancient practice of child sacrifice?

How might the author be using this narrative to exemplify the unquestioning obedience of Abraham?

What are some positive insights we can gain from this narrative?

What might be an insight or a truth from this passage that could be applied to our journeys of faith today?

## Closing

The closing is a litany prayer based on Hebrews 11:8–17, which is found on page 89. Ask members of the group to take turns reading the words based on Scripture, and invite the whole group to read in unison the prayer responses in italics.

## AFTER THE SESSION

Encourage the participants to read Genesis 24:1–67 and chapter 3 in the Participant's Guide as preparation for next week's session.

## By Faith

### A Litany
**Based on Hebrews 11:8–17**

By faith Abraham obeyed when he was called to set out for a place that he was to receive as an inheritance.

> *Gracious God, help us to be open to you when you call us away from familiar and comfortable places.*

By faith Abraham set out, not knowing where he was going.

> *Ever-present God, may we know of your presence with us when we venture into the unknown.*

By faith Abraham stayed for a time in the land he had been promised, as in a foreign land, living in tents.

> *Faithful God, grant to us a sense of hope and trust in you in those times when we find ourselves in a strange place.*

By faith Abraham looked forward to the city that has foundations, whose architect and builder is God.

> *Creator God, we praise you for the amazing works of your hand that have designed for us a world that offers us abundant gifts of food, shelter, and family.*

By faith Abraham received power of procreation, even though he was too old—and Sarah herself was barren.

> *Dependable God, by your Spirit you provide hope for those of us who have lost hope so that we may see beyond the moment into a future where you lead us.*

By faith Abraham, when put to the test, offered up Isaac. He who had received the promises was ready to offer up his only son.

> *Almighty God, when we feel ourselves being tested spiritually, emotionally, or physically, may we put our trust in you and your steadfast love toward us. Amen.*

*Session Three*

# Human Choice and Divine Purpose

*A Study of Genesis 24:1–67*

## BEFORE THE SESSION
### Focus of the Session

The focus of this session is an extended narrative in which a servant of Abraham returns to the country of Abraham's kindred to seek a wife for his son Isaac. We will deal with the concepts of divine intention, prayer, steadfast love, and hospitality that are central to the narrative and reflect on the relevance of those concepts to faith and life today.

### Advance Preparation

*   Take the time to read Genesis 24:1–67 for this session.
*   Read the comments and notes of Genesis 24 in a study Bible or commentary.

- Read articles in a Bible dictionary that deal with the concepts of "marriage," "hospitality," "prayer," and "steadfast love" in the Old Testament.

- Provide a few extra Bibles for those who forget to bring one.

## DURING THE SESSION
## Welcoming the Participants

Welcome any newcomers, give them a copy of the course book, and assure them that they will catch on quickly with the content and process. Check to see who needs to borrow a Bible and give them one, and encourage them to bring a Bible next week.

## Opening Prayer

Begin this class session with a brief prayer in which you invite the participants to contribute to the prayer in a manner similar to that used in the previous session:

- Introduce the prayer by stating that in this session we will be exploring Genesis 24, in which we read about the LORD's answer to the prayer of Abraham's servant. Comment that all prayers of petition are not always answered in the way we expect, but in this narrative about seeking a wife for Isaac, the servant's prayer was answered.

- Invite the participants to suggest times when they offered prayers of petition and they believed that their prayers were answered.

- After each suggestion is expressed, invite the group to respond in unison, "Holy God, thank you for hearing and responding to our prayers." (It will be helpful to write this response on a sheet of newsprint so that everyone can see the words.)

## Reviewing Session Two

Spend a few minutes reviewing the previous session for the sake of those who were not present and to take advantage of the reading everyone else did. Be sure not to get sidetracked in this activity because there is a lot to cover in this session. Conduct the review by doing the following:

- Start by asking, "What are some of the memorable things we discussed last week about Abraham, Sarah, and Isaac?"

- Discuss a second question: "What was the most difficult point to understand from session 2?"

- Conclude by stating, "In this session we will focus our attention on just one chapter, Genesis 24, in which we will see God at work in the midst of those whom God has blessed."

## Retelling the Story of Choosing Rebekah to Be Isaac's Wife

On pages 96–98 you will see a Readers' Theater script based on Genesis 24:1–67 that presents the narrative of Abraham's servant's seeking a wife for Isaac. It is likely that many of the class members have read the passage, but in this format they will be able to enter into the story in a more personal way. Engage the participants in the activity by the following steps:

- Invite the participants to turn to pages 96–98 in the Leader's Guide, or perhaps you have duplicated the script to distribute copies to everyone. Remind the participants that the reading is of selected verses from Genesis 24, not the complete text.

- Ask for volunteers to read the roles of narrator, Abraham, Rebekah, and Laban. The remaining members of the class will read in unison the role of the servant. (There are two reasons for this: the first is in order to involve everyone in the reading, and the second is to enable the participants to identify with a main character in the story.)

- Conduct the reading.

- After the reading, spend a few minutes commenting on some important aspects of the narrative, referring to some of the points made by the author of the Participant's Guide:

> In the time of Abraham, it was incumbent on the father to arrange for his son to be married to a woman of his own kindred.
>
> The parents usually arranged the marriages of their children.
>
> A servant acting on behalf of his master was customary.
>
> The hospitality of Rebekah's family toward the servant and his companions and camels illustrates the tradition of hospitality that was prevalent at that time among Semitic people.
>
> Giving of gifts to the bride's family was expected.
>
> The wife always went to live with the family of her husband.

- Some of these customs continue to this day among people living in the Middle East.

- Guide a discussion using one or more questions such as those that follow or those that you have prepared:

> What additional insights did you gain from this way of reading the narrative compared to your previous reading of Genesis?
>
> In what ways do you think "human choice and divine purpose" (the title of this session) is reflected in this narrative?
>
> What do you think are the key truths or understandings the author of this portion of Genesis was seeking to communicate?
>
> What truths can we discern from this narrative for our faith and life today?

## Thinking About "What If . . ." in Our Lives

A section of the Participant's Guide is titled "But What If?" (pp. 25–26). The author is referring to the servant's question regarding the consequences of his not finding a bride for Isaac who was willing to return with him to a land she had never visited to become the wife of a man she had never met. There is tension between the confidence of Abraham that the servant will be successful and the doubt of the servant regarding such success. Is it not the case that we live today with the tension between what we trust to be God's purpose and our doubts about fulfilling that purpose? Engage the participants in a few minutes of discussion, inviting them to share from their own experiences this tension between their trust in God and their doubts.

## Reflecting on the Place of Prayer

One of the pivotal moments in the narrative is when the servant prayed to the Lord to reveal to him the woman he would seek to return with him as the bride of Isaac. Make a brief presentation of what you have learned about prayer in the Old Testament. Call attention to the two appearances of an important phrase in the prayer, "steadfast love," and share some of what you have learned about this key concept in the Old Testament. Engage the class members in a time of reflection on Abraham's servant's prayer and the place of prayer today.

## Reflecting on the Theological Significance of the Story

Ask the participants to turn to the introduction to chapter 3 (pp. 23–24) where the author writes, "Humans are clearly at the center of the story, but a divine plan is being implemented. Without human participation God's purpose cannot be met. Without divine intention human activity is finally meaningless." Use this quote as a springboard for engaging the class members in a discussion guided by the questions that follow or questions you have prepared:

- What thoughts do you have about that statement?

- How would you summarize the "divine plan" that is presented by the author of the Genesis narratives we have studied so far?

- In what ways do the "divine plan" and "human activity" complement each other?

- What is your response to the statement "Without divine intention human activity is finally meaningless"?

- What are some clues that you discern regarding "divine intention" being present in the world and/or our lives today?

- What "human activity" is at work or is needed today in order for the "divine plan" to be accomplished?

## Closing

Conclude the session with the following prayer or one that you have prepared.

> Holy God, we praise and thank you for creating humankind in your own image in order to have an eternal relationship with you. Help us to be open to the lead-ing of your Spirit in our lives so that we may do our part in helping to fulfill your divine plan for our lives and our world. We celebrate your steadfast love that empowers and sustains us every moment of our lives. In your holy name we pray. Amen.

## AFTER THE SESSION

Encourage the participants to read Genesis 25:1–28:9 and chapter 4 in the Participant's Guide as preparation for next week's session.

## Readers' Theater: The Search for a Wife for Isaac

Genesis 24 (selected verses)

Narrator: Now Abraham was old, well advanced in years; and the LORD had blessed Abraham in all things. He said to his servant,

Abraham: "Put your hand under my thigh and I will make you swear by the LORD, the God of heaven and earth, that you will not get a wife for my son from the daughters of the Canaanites, among whom I live, but will go to my country and to my kindred and get a wife for my son Isaac."

Servant: "Perhaps the woman may not be willing to follow me to this land; must I then take your son back to the land from which you came?"

Abraham: "See to it that you do not take my son back there. The LORD, the God of heaven, who took me from my father's house and from the land of my birth, and who spoke to me and swore to me, 'To your offspring I will give this land,' he will send his angel before you, and you shall take a wife for my son from there.

Narrator: Then the servant took ten of his master's camels and departed, taking all kinds of choice gifts from his master; and he set out and went to Aram-naharaim, to the city of Nahor. He made the camels kneel down outside the city by the well of water; it was toward evening, the time when women go out to draw water.

Servant: "O LORD, God of my master Abraham, please grant me success today and show steadfast love to my master Abraham. I am standing here by the spring of water, and the daughters of the townspeople are coming out to draw water. Let the girl to whom I shall say, 'Please offer your jar that I may drink,' and who shall say, 'Drink, and I will water your camels'—let her be the one whom you have appointed for your servant Isaac. By this I shall know that you have shown steadfast love to my master."

Narrator: Before he had finished speaking, there was Rebekah, who was born to Bethuel son of Milcah, the wife of Nahor, Abraham's brother, coming out with her water jar on her shoulder. The girl was very fair to look upon, a virgin, whom no man had known. She went down to the spring, filled her jar, and came up. Then the servant ran to meet her and said,

Servant: "Please let me sip a little water from your jar."

Rebekah: "Drink, my lord."

Narrator: When she had finished giving him a drink, she said,

## Readers' Theater: The Search for a Wife for Isaac *(continued)*

| | |
|---|---|
| Rebekah: | "I will draw for your camels also, until they have finished drinking." |
| Narrator: | So she quickly emptied her jar into the trough and ran again to the well to draw, and she drew for all his camels. The man gazed at her in silence to learn whether or not the LORD had made his journey successful. |
| Servant: | "Tell me whose daughter you are. Is there room in your father's house for us to spend the night?" |
| Rebekah: | "I am the daughter of Bethuel son of Milcah, whom she bore to Nahor. We have plenty of straw and fodder and a place to spend the night." |
| Servant: | "Blessed be the LORD, the God of my master Abraham, who has not forsaken his steadfast love and his faithfulness toward my master. As for me, the LORD has led me on the way to the house of my master's kin." |
| Narrator: | Then the girl ran and told her mother's household about these things. Rebekah had a brother whose name was Laban; and Laban ran out to the man, to the spring. |
| Laban: | "Come in, O blessed of the LORD. Why do you stand outside when I have prepared the house and a place for the camels?" |
| Narrator: | So the man came into the house; and Laban unloaded the camels, and gave him straw and fodder for the camels, and water to wash his feet and the feet of the men who were with him. Then food was set before him to eat. |
| Servant: | "I will not eat until I have told my errand." |
| Laban: | "Speak on." |
| Servant: | "I am Abraham's servant. The LORD has greatly blessed my master, and he has become wealthy. And Sarah my master's wife bore a son to my master when she was old. I came today to the spring, and said, 'O LORD, the God of my master Abraham, if now you will only make successful the way I am going! Before I had finished speaking in my heart, there was Rebekah coming out with her water jar on her shoulder; and she went down to the spring, and drew. I said to her, 'Please let me drink.' She quickly let down her jar from her shoulder, and said, 'Drink, and I will also water your camels.' So I drank, and she also watered the camels. Then I bowed my head and worshiped the LORD, and blessed the LORD, the God of my master Abraham, who had led me by the right way to obtain the daughter of my master's kinsman for his son. Now then, if you will deal loyally and truly with my master, tell me; and if not, tell me, so that I may turn either to the right hand or to the left." |

## Readers' Theater: The Search for a Wife for Isaac *(continued)*

| | |
|---|---|
| Laban: | "The thing comes from the LORD; we cannot speak to you anything bad or good. Look, Rebekah is before you, take her and go, and let her be the wife of your master's son, as the LORD has spoken." |
| Narrator: | When Abraham's servant heard their words, he bowed himself to the ground before the LORD. And the servant brought out jewelry of silver and of gold, and garments, and gave them to Rebekah; he also gave to her brother and to her mother costly ornaments. Then he and the men who were with him ate and drank, and they spent the night there. When they rose in the morning, he said, |
| Servant: | "Send me back to my master." |
| Laban: | "Let the girl remain with us a while, at least ten days; after that she may go." |
| Servant: | "Do not delay me, since the LORD has made my journey successful; let me go that I may go to my master." |
| Laban: | "We will call the girl, and ask her." |
| Narrator: | And they called Rebekah. |
| Laban: | "Will you go with this man?" |
| Rebekah: | "I will." |
| Narrator: | So they sent away their sister Rebekah and her nurse along with Abraham's servant and his men. And they blessed Rebekah and said to her, |
| Laban: | "May you, our sister, become thousands of myriads; may your offspring gain possession of the gates of their foes." |
| Narrator: | Then Rebekah and her maids rose up, mounted the camels, and followed the man; thus the servant took Rebekah, and went his way. Now Isaac had come from Beer-lahai-roi, and was settled in the Negeb. Isaac went out in the evening to walk in the field; and looking up, he saw camels coming. And Rebekah looked up, and when she saw Isaac, she slipped quickly from the camel, and said to the servant, |
| Rebekah: | "Who is the man over there, walking in the field to meet us?" |
| Servant: | "It is my master." |
| Narrator: | So she took her veil and covered herself. And the servant told Isaac all the things that he had done. Then Isaac brought her into his mother Sarah's tent. He took Rebekah, and she became his wife; and he loved her. So Isaac was comforted after his mother's death. |

# Passing On the Promise

## *A Study of Genesis 25:1–28:9*

### BEFORE THE SESSION
### Focus of the Session

The focus of this session is on what the author of the Participant's Guide describes as a "dysfunctional family." The four key characters of the family are Isaac, Rebekah, Esau, and Jacob. We will explore something of the strengths and weaknesses of each of the family members as well as reflect on the concepts of "birthright "and "blessing" that are central to the larger narrative.

### Advance Preparation

- Take the time to read Genesis 25:1–28:9 for this session.

- Read the comments and notes for Genesis 25–28 in a study Bible or commentary.

- Read articles in a Bible dictionary and notes in a study Bible that deal with the concepts of "birthright" and "blessing."

- Find brief articles in a Bible dictionary or other resource featuring personalities of the Bible. Copy and duplicate excerpts from articles on Isaac, Rebekah, Esau, and Jacob as resources for the participants to use in the "Exploring Four Main Characters" activity.

- Provide a few extra Bibles for those who forget to bring one.

## DURING THE SESSION
## Welcoming the Participants

Arrive at class early enough to set up the refreshments and to have everything ready before the first persons arrive. Greet each one by name with a warm welcome. Welcome any newcomers, give them a copy of the course book, and assure them that they will catch on quickly with the content and process. Check to see who needs to borrow a Bible, and give them one, and encourage everyone to bring a Bible next week.

## Opening Prayer

Begin this class session with a prayer using selected verses from Psalm 71.

- Introduce the prayer by stating that the book of Psalms was the first prayer book of God's people. Though the psalms were composed in a particular time very different from our own, they are mysteriously contemporary, so some of them can be our prayers as well as the psalmist's.

- Locate the prayer in the Leader's Guide, page 106.

- Invite the participants to pray the prayer responsively with half of the class speaking the plain-text lines and the other half the indented lines in italics.

## Reviewing Session Three

Spend a few minutes reviewing the previous session for the sake of those who were not present and to take advantage of the reading everyone else did. Be sure not to get sidetracked in this activity because there is a lot to cover in this session. Conduct the review by doing the following:

- Start by asking those who were present to recall the main points of the narrative that was the focus of the previous week.

- Prompt a discussion by asking, "What were the central truths that were communicated by the writer of Genesis in the story of Abraham's seeking a wife for Isaac?"

- Conclude the discussion with another question: "What insights from the narrative can be applied to our faith and life today?"

## Exploring Four Main Characters

The four key characters in this session's narrative are Isaac, Rebekah, Esau, and Jacob. In this activity the class will work in four small groups with each group focusing on just one character. You need to use a Bible dictionary and/or a book that features Bible personalities to find brief articles with background material on each of the characters. Duplicate about one page of information for each character for the small groups to use for research.

- Divide the class into four small groups and assign each group one of the four characters: Isaac, Rebekah, Esau, and Jacob.

- Direct the participants to "Exploring Four Key Characters in a Dysfunctional Family" on p. 107.

- Distribute the appropriate information sheets to their respective groups.

- Allow about fifteen minutes for the groups to read their information sheets and to discuss the four questions.

- Next, rearrange the participants into groups of four, with each group having participants who represent each of the four characters. (If there are an uneven number of persons, it will be OK for two persons to represent one or more of the four characters.)

• In the new groups of four, each person will share his or her answers to the four questions related to the character their group focused on.

• After about five minutes of sharing in the groups of four, reconvene as a whole group and spend a few more minutes discussing the following questions or those you prepared:

> What insights have come to you as you considered the interactions between these four persons in a dysfunctional family?

> What does the inclusion of such stories in the Bible suggest to you about the motivations of the writers of Genesis?

> How do these narratives contribute to "passing on the promise"?

> What is the relevance of such narratives in Genesis to our relationship with God and one another today?

## Reflecting on Narratives of Birthright and Blessings

The four narratives in the portion of Genesis that is the focus of this session revolve around the concepts of birthright and blessing: (1) Esau forfeits his birthright to Jacob (25:29–34); (2) Rebekah and Jacob conspire to deceive Isaac into giving his blessing to Jacob (27:1–29); (3) Esau receives a blessing from Isaac (27:30–40); and (4) Jacob receives a second blessing from Isaac (28:1–5). In this part of the session your goal is to enable the class members to review the four narratives, to discern the meaning of the concepts "birthright" and "blessing," and to relate those concepts to faith and life today.

Begin by directing the participants' attention to Genesis 25:29–34, the story of Esau's forfeiting his birthright to Jacob. After reviewing the main actions in the narrative offer the following comments:

• A birthright is a special honor granted to the firstborn son in which he receives a double portion of the family's inheritance and eventually becomes the patriarch of the family or tribe. Other sons receive a portion of the inheritance, but the oldest son receives a double portion.

- The eldest son can sell or give away his birthright but in so doing forfeits any claim to the family's fortune or the leadership role as the patriarch of the family or tribe.

- Esau's claim of his birthright was trumped by his momentary desire to satisfy a need for food.

- "Thus Esau despised his birthright" (25:34) is a very strong statement that summarizes the author's perspective on Esau.

Move to the next narrative (Gen. 27:1–29) that provides an account of how Rebekah and Jacob conspired to deceive Isaac into giving a blessing to Jacob instead of to the rightful recipient, Esau. Invite the participants to retell the story without referring to their Bibles. You may need to fill in some of the gaps or to straighten out the story line if parts of it are suggested out of sequence. Continue by presenting some background information that you have gleaned from your reading of a Bible commentary or notes in a study Bible. Be sure to emphasize the following:

- Prior to the death of his father the oldest son would receive a blessing from his father.

- Even though Esau forfeited his birthright, he was still due his father's blessing prior to Isaac's death.

- Behind this scene of deception on the part of Rebekah and Jacob is the reality, in the writer's mind, that the God of Abraham is the one who gives the ultimate blessing.

- The blessing consists of riches from the land and the subjugation of other peoples, including the brothers.

- In the times of Isaac, Esau, and Jacob, a man's word was binding. Once a blessing is given it is impossible to withdraw it or take it back.

Isaac gave a second blessing (Gen. 27:30–40), this time to Esau after he discovers he has been cheated out of the blessing he was due. There are several elements of this passage worth calling attention to:

- Isaac was greatly troubled as a result of being duped by Jacob; "Then Isaac trembled violently" (27:33).

- Even so, Isaac was bound by custom to keep his word by allowing the blessing of Jacob to stand.

- Esau persists in seeking a blessing from his father, who does offer a blessing but not the one Esau desired. Read again Genesis 27:38–40.

- Isaac's blessing reveals that Esau will not benefit from "the fatness of the earth," that he will have to live by the sword, and that he will have to serve his brother.

The final blessing given by Isaac is again to Jacob (28:1–5). Rebekah is aware of Esau's hatred toward Jacob and his vow to kill his brother after the death of Isaac and a time of mourning. Rebekah advises Jacob to go to Haran to find a woman of her kinfolk to marry. She also intercedes with Isaac to speak with Jacob on the matter. Thus Isaac called Jacob to come to him and gave him both a charge and a blessing. The charge was not to marry a Canaanite woman but to return to Rebekah's brother Laban to marry one of his daughters. And the blessing was "'May God Almighty bless you and make you fruitful and numerous . . . that you may take possession of the land . . . that God gave to Abraham'" (28:3, 4). Note the following points:

- Isaac and his family are living as aliens in the land of the Canaanites, which is the land promised to Abraham and his descendents. However, they do not yet possess the land.

- In order for God's promise to be passed from one generation to the next it is necessary that Jacob find a wife among Abraham's and Rebekah's Aramean kinfolk in Haran.

- Even today there are strong customs among people of the Middle East to marry within one's own kinship group in order to maintain the customs of social position, family status, ethnic identity, and property ownership.

- Much of the struggle between Jews and Arabs in Israel and Palestine today revolves around these very customs.

## Guiding a Group Discussion

We have explored and reflected on a series of narratives that are intricately woven together to create a larger narrative in which the author shows God at work among the people of God's choosing. Wrap up the class period with a discussion guided by questions such as those that follow or ones you have created.

- What are some of your impressions regarding the writer's storytelling abilities in terms of how the issues are presented and the characters are treated?

- In the narratives of Isaac, Rebekah, Esau, and Jacob we are introduced to a variety of dynamics in family relationships. What are some examples of family relationships today that are somewhat similar to what we read in Genesis?

- The author of the Participant's Guide writes, "The human characters in the divine story are far from perfect, brave, moral folk. They are rather quite selfish at times and very untrusting of God's guidance. But at the same time . . . the story underscores . . . that the divine purpose is continued despite what human characters may do" (p. 35). What are some responses you would make to that statement?

- To what extent do you think there is a "divine purpose" at work in the world today?

- What do you believe is the "divine purpose" at work in your own faith and life?

## Closing

Conclude the session by reading from Psalm 105:7–11. Psalm 105 is sometimes identified as a Psalm of God's Mighty Acts, meaning that the words of the psalmist recount in summary fashion some of God's acts of deliverance on behalf of the people of God. These five verses summarize the roles of Abraham, Isaac, and Jacob. Follow the psalm reading with a brief prayer in which you offer praise and thanksgiving for God's gracious acts of covenant, blessing, and salvation.

## AFTER THE SESSION

Encourage the participants to read Genesis 28:10–32:32 and chapter 5 in the Participant's Guide as preparation for next week's session.

## A Psalmist's Prayer and Our Prayer

(Based on Selected Verses of Psalm 71)

In you, O LORD, I take refuge; for you are my rock and my fortress.

*For you, O Lord, are my hope, my trust, O LORD, from my youth.*

Upon you I have leaned from my birth; it was you who took me from my mother's womb.

*My praise is continually of you.*

My mouth will tell of your righteous acts, of your deeds of salvation all day long, though their number is past my knowledge.

*I will come praising the mighty deeds of the Lord GOD, I will praise your righteousness, yours alone.*

O God, from my youth you have taught me, and I still proclaim your wondrous deeds.

*So even to old age and gray hairs, O God, do not forsake me, until I proclaim your might to all the generations to come.*

Your power and your righteousness, O God, reach the high heavens.

*I will also praise you with the harp for your faithfulness, O my God;*

I will sing praises to you with the lyre, O Holy One of Israel.

*My lips will shout for joy when I sing praises to you; my soul also, which you have rescued.*

Amen.

| Exploring Four Key Characters in a Dysfunctional Family | | | | |
|---|---|---|---|---|
| | Isaac | Rebekah | Jacob | Esau |
| 1. What are his/her admirable traits? | | | | |
| 2. What are his/her less-than-admirable traits? | | | | |
| 3. What might he/she have wished to be different? | | | | |
| 4. What, for you, is most memorable about this person? | | | | |

*Session Five*

# Mystery Surrounds the Ordinary

*A Study of Genesis 28:10–32:32*

## BEFORE THE SESSION
### Focus of the Session

The focus of this session is an extended narrative that features four key personalities: Jacob, Laban, and Laban's two daughters, Leah and Rachel. There are two encounters that Jacob has with God that precede and follow Jacob's time in Haran. Throughout the session you will be aiming to help the class members connect with the narratives experientially.

### Advance Preparation

- Take the time to read Genesis 28:10–32:32 for this session.

- Read the comments and notes of Genesis 28–32 in a study Bible or commentary.

- Prepare a sheet of newsprint with the response the participants will say as part of the closing litany prayer.

- Provide a few extra Bibles for those who forget to bring one.

## DURING THE SESSION
## Opening Prayer

The opening prayer focuses on the words of Psalm 63 as presented in the *Today's English Version* of the Bible, also known as the *Good News Bible*. The words to guide the prayer are from Psalm 63:1–4.

> *O God, you are my God, and I long for you.*
> *My whole being desires you.*
> *Like a dry, worn-out, and waterless land,*
> *My soul is thirsty for you.*
> *Let me see you in the sanctuary.*
> *Let me see how mighty and glorious you are.*
> *Your constant love is better than life itself,*
> *And so I will praise you.*
> *I will give you thanks as long as I live.*
> *I will raise my hands to you in prayer.*

Lead the psalm prayer in the following process:

- Introduce the prayer you will lead as one from Psalm 63:1–4.

- Invite the class members to repeat the words prayerfully as you speak them a line at a time.

- Pray each of the lines above, one at a time, followed by the participants' repeating that line.

- Next, direct them to turn to this page of the Leader's Guide and ask them to read the words again in order to select one or two lines that "speak" in a special way to them at this moment.

- Then, invite the participants to share the lines they have chosen.

- After those who desire to share have done so, invite the whole group to pray all the lines of the psalm again in unison.

## Reviewing Session Four

Spend a few minutes reviewing the previous session for the sake of those who were not present and to make the transition to this week's topic. Conduct the review by doing the following:

- Start by asking those who were present last week to summarize key characteristics of the four main characters in the narrative: Isaac, Rebekah, Esau, and Jacob.

- Prompt a brief discussion by asking, "What were the most significant things you learned from these stories about a 'dysfunctional family'?"

- Conclude the discussion with another question: "What do these narratives tell us about God's 'divine purpose'?"

## Reflecting on Jacob's Encounter with God at Bethel

Before dealing with the narrative of Jacob's dream at Bethel, invite class members to discuss some of their impressions of or experiences with dreams. It is not necessary for them to share details of their dreams but to share what they think about the importance (or lack thereof) of dreams in their lives.

Next, turn to page 41 of the Participant's Guide and read together the paragraph that begins, "During the night Jacob had a dream." Spend a few minutes reflecting together on the author's words.

Next spend a few minutes focusing on the narrative in Genesis 28:10–22. Guide the group through the reading by calling attention to some significant points:

- On the advice of Rebekah and following a charge from Isaac, Jacob heads off toward Haran, the home of his grandfather, Abraham, and his mother.

- There is no textual evidence to suggest that Jacob has any companions on his journey, but whether he was accompanied by anyone on the trip or not does not affect the import of his encounter with God.

- Notice the footnotes in the NRSV that give alternative renderings of "stairway" and "ramp" for the Hebrew word that is translated "ladder."

- Jacob has two encounters with God in the larger passage for this session, Genesis 28:10–32:32, which serve as brackets, or bookends, for the whole narrative. The first encounter is here, as Jacob departs Canaan to go to Haran. The second encounter is when he returns and is about to reenter Canaan.

- Haran is several hundred miles to the north.

- In *The New Interpreter's Study Bible,* Theodore Hiebert writes in the study notes for this passage, "These two encounters . . . are sacred portals for his exit from and entry into the promised land, signifying God's presence with him on his journey" (p. 53).

- Jacob receives the same blessing from God that was given to Abraham and Isaac before him: the promises of land, many descendants, and the blessing of many peoples (28:13–14).

- Jacob also receives a further promise: "'I am with you and will keep you wherever you go, and will bring you back to this land; for I will not leave you until I have done what I have promised you'" (28:15).

- Jacob's encounter with God must surely have been an awesome experience, which is represented by his building an altar and anointing it with oil.

- At the time of Jacob the gods of others were stationary, limited to particular places. The writer of Genesis affirms God as "on the move," present everywhere and whenever one experiences the presence of the divine.

- The name of the place, Bethel, means "house of God." Bethel becomes a sacred place that is mentioned often in the Hebrew Scriptures—seventy-five times in sixty-eight verses.

- Conclude the class's reflections on Jacob's dream at Bethel with a couple of questions:

    What do you think is the significance of God's promises to Jacob?

    No doubt this narrative reminds you of the spiritual "We Are Climbing Jacob's Ladder." What connections do you see between "climbing Jacob's ladder" and the refrain "soldiers of the cross" and

other verses like "Sinner, do you love my Jesus?"
and "If you love, him why not serve him?"

What is a place, in addition to your church, that is
for you a "Bethel," a house of God?

## Exploring the Relationships between Jacob, Laban, Leah, and Rachel

The extended narrative of this session begins with Jacob's arrival in Haran, the land of his grandfather and mother, and ends with his departure for Canaan twenty years later. The narrative is long and complex, and the interactions between Jacob, Laban, Leah, and Rachel are intriguing. Perhaps the best way to sort out the characters and their relationships with one another is to use a process similar to the last session when the class worked in four groups, each group focusing on a different person. Use the following process to guide your class:

- Divide the class into four small groups, and assign each group one of the four characters: Jacob, Laban, Leah, and Rachel.

- Direct the class members to page 116 to the worksheet with suggested readings for each character and three discussion questions.

- Allow about fifteen minutes for the groups to read their assigned Genesis passages and to discuss the questions.

- Next, rearrange the participants into groups of four, with each person representing one of the four characters. (If there is an uneven number of persons, it will be OK for two persons to represent one or more of the four characters.)

- In the new groups of four, each participant will take on the role of the person he/she focused on. Speaking in the first person, participants are to interact with one another guided by one question: "What are your feelings toward the other three members of the family and about what has happened to you?"

- After about five minutes of sharing in the groups of four, reconvene as a whole group and spend a few more minutes discussing the following questions or those you prepared:

Say a little bit about your experience of identifying with the role of one of the four main characters of the narrative.

What are some of the cultural realities reflected in these Genesis passages that are quite different from our cultural norms today?

When you consider the whole of the narrative, what do you sense the writer was trying to communicate to believers?

In what ways do you see this narrative having relevance for faith and life today?

## Considering Jacob's Second Encounter with God

The concluding short narrative of this session is where Jacob finds himself wrestling with an unnamed opponent for the whole night. Ask someone to read, or the group could read in unison, Genesis 32:22–32. Follow the reading by calling attention to several important points:

- Jacob sent on ahead his wives, children, flocks, and all that was his. He was left alone.

- The Jabbok was a stream that flowed from the highlands of the east into the Jordan River and was known later as the boundary between Israel and the Ammonites.

- Jacob's opponent in the all-night wrestling match is unnamed. However, he is identified both as a man (v. 25) and as God (v. 30).

- Neither of the opponents is a clear victor in the struggle. The unnamed man (God) only injures Jacob, but he also blesses him with a new name. Jacob, though injured, is said to have "striven with God and with humans and [to] have prevailed" (32:28)

- Jacob's name being changed to Israel is significant, as are all names and name changes in the Bible. The name "Israel" means "one who strives with God," which in addition to being associated with this particular event is relevant for all of the nations of Israel's history.

- Jacob inquires about the name of his opponent, but the name is not revealed to him. Instead, the opponent blesses Jacob.

- After being given a new name and being blessed by the opponent, Jacob, now known as Israel, says, "'I have seen God face to face, and yet my life is preserved'" (32:30). It was believed that if one saw the face of God, one would die.

- Conclude your reflection on Jacob's second encounter with God with discussion guided by a couple of questions:

    What do you think is the significance of the name change and the meaning of the new name Israel?

    Why do you suppose the writer left it ambiguous as to who was the victor of the wrestling match?

    What experiences have you had where you felt like you were wrestling with an issue, challenge, or decision to make, and you received a blessing from God?

    Which part of the narrative inspires you the most?

## Closing

If you are running short of time, you could offer a closing prayer that expresses to God praise and thanksgiving for God's steadfast love. Or you could use the following brief litany as your closing. Speak the following four "words of the LORD" (based on Gen. 28:13–15),and ask the participants to respond in unison, "O God, your steadfast love is an awesome blessing." (Be sure to write out the response on a sheet of newsprint and post it where everyone can see.)

- The Lord said to Jacob, "I am the LORD, the God of Abraham your father and the God of Isaac." (Response)

- The Lord said to Jacob, "All the families of the earth shall be blessed in you and in your offspring." (Response)

- The Lord said to Jacob, "Know that I am with you and will keep you wherever you go." (Response)

- The Lord said to Jacob, "I will not leave you until I have done what I have promised you." (Response)

## AFTER THE SESSION

Encourage the participants to read Genesis 33:1–36:43 and chapter 6 in the Participant's Guide as preparation for next week's session.

| Jacob, Laban, and Two Daughters | | | |
|---|---|---|---|
| | **Jacob** Gen. 29:10–14, 18–26, 30; 30:25–32; 31:1–7, 22–31, 43–55 | **Laban** Gen. 29:13–18, 21–26; 30:25–32; 31:1–7, 22–31, 43–55 | **Leah** Gen. 29:21–26, 31–35; 30:18–21 | **Rachel** Gen. 29:9–12, 28–30; 30:1–8, 22–24 |
| 1. What do you sense to be his/ her motives or desires? | | | | |
| 2. What do you see as his/her feelings toward self, God, and/ or the other three characters? | | | | |
| 3. What, for you, is most memo- rable about this person? | | | | |

*Session Six*

# Loose Ends

*A Study of Genesis 33:1–36:43*

## BEFORE THE SESSION
### Focus of the Session

This session focuses on a series of narratives that the author of the Participant's Guide refers to as "loose ends." We will encounter events where the divine presence is experienced by Jacob, along with events where a shameful side of human nature expresses itself in violence. We will read about the birth of Benjamin and the death of Rachel, and the narrative identifies the sons of Jacob along with the sons of Esau and their families. We will be exploring a complex four chapters.

### Advance Preparation

- Take the time to read Genesis 33:1–36:43 for this session.

- Read the comments and notes of Genesis 33–36 in a study Bible or commentary.

- Prepare a sheet of newsprint with the response to the opening litany prayer, or write it on a whiteboard.

- Provide a few extra Bibles for those who forget to bring one.

- Arrange to bring to class hymnals with the words to "Our God, Our Help in Ages Past" for singing as the closing, or duplicate copies of the words to the hymn.

## DURING THE SESSION
## Opening Prayer

Psalm 121 will provide the focus for this session's opening prayer. The psalm expresses trust and confidence in God, who is identified as a "keeper" of the faithful, and the word "keep" appears five times in eight verses. Guide the class members in a litany prayer by the following process:

- Introduce Psalm 121 as a hymn of trust and confidence by sharing any insights you have gained from a study Bible or commentary.

- Tell the group that their response to each verse will be the words from the first half of the second verse, "My help comes from the LORD."

- Read Psalm 121:1–8, and pause after each verse for the participants to respond.

- After sharing Psalm 121, discuss the following question: "What are some ways you have experienced your help coming from the LORD?"

## Reviewing Session Five

Spend a few minutes reviewing the previous session for the sake of those who were not present and to make the transition to this week's topic. Conduct the review by doing the following:

- Start by asking those who were present last week to summarize the key events in Jacob's journey from Canaan, his years in Haran, and his return to Canaan.

• Spend a few minutes discussing one question: "What have we learned about the customs of the people in the time of Jacob?"

## Summarizing the Narratives

With the participants, skim through Genesis 33:1–36:43 to review the sequence of events, the key personalities, and the locations described in the narrative. Direct them to pages 123–24, where there are two maps that show the key locations mentioned in the narrative. Be sure to include the following:

• Jacob travels from Haran in the north, and Esau, from Edom in the south.

• They meet somewhere east of the Jordan River and north of Succoth.

• Jacob goes ahead of his family and flocks to meet Esau, wherein they embrace and kiss.

• There is an extended exchange between the brothers concluding with an agreement for Esau to return to Seir (Edom) in the south and Jacob to move to Shechem to the west.

• Jacob purchases land in Canaan from Hamor, Shechem's father.

• Dinah, the daughter of Jacob and Leah, is raped by Shechem.

• Hamor and Jacob agree that Dinah will be given to be Shechem's wife and that their two families will share the land together.

• Two of Jacob's sons, Simeon and Levi, avenge the rape of their sister by slaughtering all the men of Hamor's family.

• Jacob rebukes his sons for their evil deed.

• Jacob returns to Bethel, where he receives the blessing from God a second time.

• Rachel dies during the birth of her son Benjamin and is buried "on the way to Ephrath (that is, Bethlehem)" (Gen. 35:19).

- Isaac dies and is buried by Jacob and Esau in Hebron.

- Genesis 36 is an accounting of the descendents of Esau.

## Exploring Jacob's Reunion with Esau

Before looking at the narrative of the reunion of Jacob and Esau, guide the class to recall the events that caused the estrangement between the two brothers. Then ask, "Given human nature, what do you think would be an expected outcome of Jacob's meeting with Esau?"

Instead of Esau's seeking revenge for the wrong done to him by Jacob, he "ran to meet him, and embraced him, and fell on his neck and kissed him, and they wept" (33:4). Theodore Hiebert writes in his notes for this passage in *The New Interpreter's Study Bible*, "The story endorses reconciliation rather than violence as the proper resolution of conflict both within the family, as represented by the brothers Jacob and Esau, and between nations, as represented by their descendents, the Israelites and the Edomites" (p. 60).

Spend a few minutes discussing this narrative and some insights that can be applied to faith and life today:

- What do you think are the main points the writer is seeking to communicate through this narrative of Jacob and Esau's reunion?

- What are some other passages in the Bible where reconciliation "trumps" revenge?

- Why is it so hard in our own family or community experiences to take steps toward reconciliation when there are severe grievances between the parties?

- If you have had an experience of reuniting with a long-separated family member, what were the before-and-after experiences like for you?

- What makes family reunions special and or sometimes difficult?

## Considering the Rape of Dinah

Genesis 34, the focus of this activity, and Genesis 33, the focus of our previous activity, represent a startling contrast. The deceit of Jacob's taking Esau's birthright and blessing from him that was perpetrated by him and his mother,

Rebekah, was made right many years later by the reunion of Jacob and Esau. The brothers experienced reconciliation even though Esau had every reason to seek revenge against Jacob. On the other hand, just a few verses later we read the account of a daughter of Jacob, Dinah, who is raped by Shechem, the son of Hamor, for which two sons of Jacob, Simeon and Levi, exact revenge by slaughtering all the men of Hamor's family. Hamor and Jacob had negotiated a solution to the violent act of Shechem but were not able to settle the account because of the vengeful acts of Simeon and Levi. There is a startling contrast between the outcomes of these two side-by-side narratives where, on the one hand, reconciliation reigns and, on the other hand, revenge is achieved.

The rape of Dinah is a difficult narrative to discuss because of the nature of the violence done to her and because of the slaughter of all the men of her family. Yet within the narrative there is an attempt on the part of Hamor and Jacob to achieve a settlement that would be in the best interest of everyone. But, as often is the case in biblical narratives as well as our own personal narratives, good intentions are often undercut by the actions of others beyond our control. Guide the discussion among class members with the questions that follow or those you have prepared:

- If you had been an editor assembling the multiple narratives of Genesis, what would have been your rationale for either excluding or including this narrative as part of the whole?

- Why do you suppose those who gathered into one collection of narratives the book we know as Genesis included this narrative?

- In what ways does this narrative show what is admirable as well as what is shameful about human nature?

- What in this narrative would hint that God's promise to Jacob was being fulfilled?

- What are some examples in our world today where revenge, like that taken by Jacob's sons, seems to take precedence over conciliatory acts like those of Jacob and Hamor?

## Reflecting on More "Loose Ends"

Genesis 35 contains several more "loose ends" as identified by the author of the Participant's Guide: Jacob's return to Bethel, the revelation of names for God, the birth of Benjamin, the death of Rachel, and the death of Isaac. In order to work with this chapter, guide the group in the following process:

- Divide the class into groups of four. (If the class members do not divide equally into groups of four, it will be OK to have groups of three.)

- Assign each of the four members of a group a different portion of Genesis 35 (1–8, 9–15, 16–21, and 22–29).

- Ask each person to read the passage assigned to him or her and to reflect on the three questions/tasks related to the passage listed in the worksheet on page 125.

- Allow about five minutes for the individuals to read their assigned passages and reflect on the questions/ tasks, and then direct them to share the insights they gained with the other three persons in their group.

- When the small groups are finished, return as a total group, and spend a few minutes discussing the following questions or ones you have planned:

  > What do you sense is the overarching message the author of Genesis is seeking to communicate?

  > What relevance, if any, do you see of these passages to our faith today?

## Closing

The words to the Isaac Watts hymn "Our God, Our Help in Ages Past" are an appropriate way to bring closure to this session. If the class members know the tune and some are comfortable singing without accompaniment, sing one or more of the five verses. If the group is too small to sing or they are not comfortable singing, then read the words to the hymn in unison as your closing prayer.

## AFTER THE SESSION

Encourage the participants to read Genesis 37:1–50:26 and chapter 7 in the Participant's Guide as preparation for next week's session.

Fig. 1: Sites Mentioned in Genesis 33–35

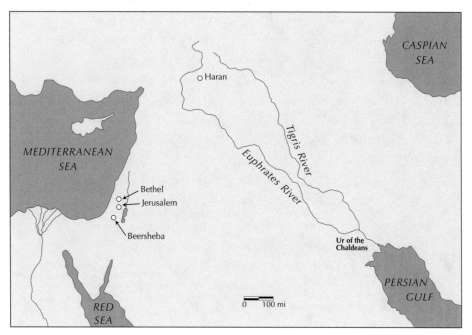

Fig. 2: Sites Mentioned in Genesis 33–35

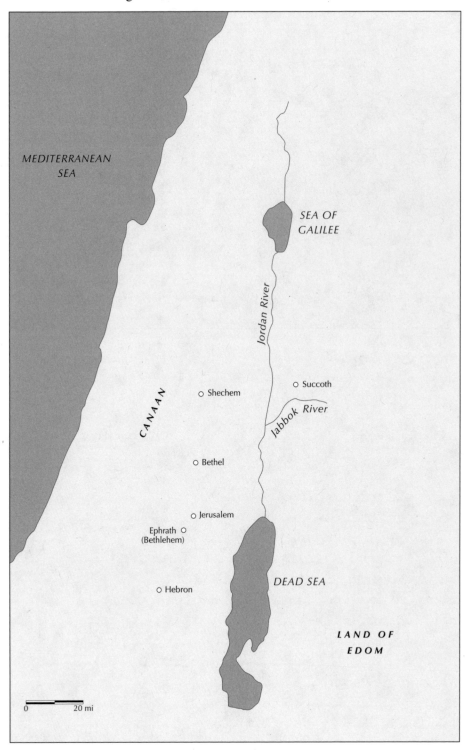

## Loose Ends in Genesis 35:1–29

|  | Questions/Tasks to Consider |
|---|---|
| **Genesis 35:1–8** | 1. Notice the locations mentioned in the passage, and find them on the map.<br><br>2. What do you see as the significance of Jacob's being directed to Bethel and meeting God there?<br><br>3. What is the significance of Jacob's erecting an altar? |
| **Genesis 35:9–15** | 1. Notice the name for God in 35:11 and the NRSV footnote.<br><br>2. What do you think is the significance of Jacob's receiving a blessing from God a second time?<br><br>3. What is the significance of Jacob's setting up a pillar and anointing it with oil? |
| **Genesis 35:16–21** | 1. Notice the locations mentioned in the passage, and find on the map the ones that are listed.<br><br>2. What do you see as the significance of Rachel's dying at the time of Benjamin's birth?<br><br>3. What is the significance of Jacob's erecting a pillar at Rachel's grave? |
| **Genesis 35:22–29** | 1. Notice the locations mentioned in the passage, and find them on the map.<br><br>2. What do you sense to be the significance of the burial place for Isaac?<br><br>3. What is the significance of Esau and Jacob's burying Isaac? |

*Session Seven*

# The Providence of God

*A Study of Genesis 37:1–50:26*

## BEFORE THE SESSION
### Focus of the Session

The focus of this session is the final fourteen chapters of the book of Genesis. Joseph is the central character of these fourteen chapters, but there are many others with prominent roles: his father, Jacob; his brothers; Potiphar; Potiphar's wife; and Pharaoh. Through the major activity in the middle of the session participants will have opportunity to gain an overview of the larger narrative and to connect to it in a personal way.

### Advance Preparation

- Take the time to read Genesis 37:1–50:26 for this session.

- Read the comments and notes of Genesis 37–50 in a study Bible or commentary.

- If you choose to use the suggestion for the opening prayer, you will need to secure a CD of Andrew Lloyd Webber's musical *Joseph and the Amazing Technicolor Dreamcoat* or purchase and download from iTunes the "Prologue" of the musical.

- Prepare a sheet of newsprint with the response to the closing litany prayer, or write it on a whiteboard.

- Provide a few extra Bibles for those who forget to bring one.

## DURING THE SESSION
### Opening Prayer

Consider using a musical introduction to this opening prayer by playing the "Prologue" from Andrew Lloyd Webber's popular musical *Joseph and the Amazing Technicolor Dreamcoat*. The lyrics by Tim Rice include "Some folks dream of the wonders they'll do. . . . We all dream a lot. / Some are lucky, some are not." Guide the class through the following process:

- Ask how many have seen the musical and/or how many know the lyrics for some of the songs of the musical.

- Introduce the musical and the words of the "Prologue" that will introduce our opening prayer.

- Listen to the "Prologue," which will take less than two minutes.

- Discuss briefly one question: "What do you make of the contrast between the title of this session, 'The Providence of God,' and the words of the song, 'We all dream a lot. / Some are lucky, some are not'?"

- Conclude with a brief prayer of petition that God will guide and inspire everyone in the process of the class's exploration of the Joseph narratives in Genesis.

### Reviewing Session Six

Spend a few minutes reviewing the previous session for the sake of those who were not present and to make the transition to this week's topic. Conduct the review by doing the following:

- Start by asking those who were present last week to summarize the key events involving Jacob, Esau, Dinah, Shechem, Rachel, Benjamin, and Isaac.

- Spend a few minutes discussing one question: "What loose ends remain for you regarding the narratives studied last week?"

## Summarizing the Extended Narrative

The Joseph narrative comprises the last fourteen chapters of Genesis. There are so many subplots in the narrative that it is not possible to study in depth all fourteen chapters in this one session. This activity will be the major activity of the session, so be sure to allow enough time for the class members to complete the tasks outlined in the following steps:

- Direct the class members to the worksheet on page 131, "Twenty Major Episodes in Genesis 37–50."

- Assign each person one of the episodes and its related verses. (If you do not have twenty persons, either combine several of the events or eliminate as many as necessary. Another option, if your class is ten or fewer, is to plan for this session to take two weeks. If you have more than twenty, it would work to assign two or more persons to an episode.)

- Ask each person to read his or her assigned verses and to make note of the key persons, events, and words featured in the passage.

- After time for reading ask the class members to retell the story in their own words. Encourage them not to read the passage from their Bibles but to use their creative imaginations to retell their portion of the Joseph story.

## Reflecting on the Joseph Story

The retelling of the twenty episodes will probably take fifteen to twenty minutes. However long it takes is OK because this is the major activity of the session. When the retelling exercise is completed, guide the class in a discussion using questions such as those that follow or questions that you have prepared:

- Look again at your assigned passage. What, for you, is a line or verse that stands out? Share the line or verse, and state why it stands out for you.

- With what aspect of your part of the Joseph story do you personally identify?

- The title for this session is "The Providence of God." What do you understand to be the meaning of the word "providence"?

- How do you see "the providence of God" being expressed in this extended narrative of Joseph and his brothers? (See 50:15–21 as an example.)

## Evaluating the Course

You and the class have spent a number of weeks together studying the book of Genesis. You have read the Participant's Guide and many chapters in Genesis, you have participated in a variety of activities together, and you have discussed many questions. You may find it impossible to remember all that you have said and done together, but I am sure there are many things that you find memorable from your study. Take some time to wrap the course up by leading the class in discussion of as many of the following questions as you have time for:

- Of all the activities we did together, which ones were the most interesting, challenging, or helpful for you?

- What are some suggestions you would make regarding a future study like this one?

- What are some new insights or learnings that have come to you as a result of this study?

- In terms of your personal faith journey, how has this study contributed to that journey?

- Where do you hope that this study will lead you, our group, and/or our church?

## Closing

Make a transition from the above discussion to this closing activity by asking the class members to take a minute to write, or think, a completion to the sentence that begins, "God's providence is experienced as. . . . " After a minute or two of silence, invite class members to share their completed sentences. In response to each person's sentence lead the whole group to respond in unison with "Gracious God, your steadfast love endures forever." (It will be helpful to print this response on a sheet of newsprint or whiteboard for all to see.) Conclude by singing together the familiar doxology.

| Twenty Major Episodes in Genesis 37–50 | |
| --- | --- |
| 1. Trouble at Home | Gen. 37:1–4 |
| 2. A Boy with Dreams | Gen. 37:5–11 |
| 3. Thrown in a Pit | Gen. 37:12–24 |
| 4. Sold to the Ishmaelites | Gen. 37:25–36 |
| 5. Success as Potiphar's Slave | Gen. 39:1–6a |
| 6. Betrayed by Potiphar's Wife | Gen. 39:6b–18 |
| 7. Thrown into Prison | Gen. 39:19–23 |
| 8. A Prisoner with Dreams | Gen. 41:1–13 |
| 9. Interpreting Pharaoh's Dreams | Gen. 41:14–16, 25–32 |
| 10. Serving as Pharaoh's Main Man | Gen. 41:37–49 |
| 11. Jacob's Sons Seek Grain in Egypt | Gen. 42:1–9a |
| 12. Joseph and His Brothers | Gen. 42:18–25 |
| 13. A Severe Famine | Gen. 43:1–10 |
| 14. Seeing Benjamin | Gen. 43:26–34 |
| 15. Pleading for Benjamin's Release | Gen. 44:18–34 |
| 16. Joseph's Identity Revealed | Gen. 45:1–15 |
| 17. Jacob Hears Joseph Is Alive | Gen. 45:25–28 |
| 18. Jacob Settles in Egypt | Gen. 46:28–47:6 |
| 19. Jacob's Death and Burial | Gen. 49:29–50:7 |
| 20. Joseph Forgives His Brothers | Gen. 50:15–21 |

# Appendix

### Commentaries on Genesis

Arnold, Bill T. *Genesis*. The New Cambridge Bible Commentary. Cambridge: Cambridge University Press, 2009.

Brueggemann, Walter. *Genesis*. Interpretation Bible Commentary for Teaching and Preaching. Louisville, KY: Westminster John Knox Press, 1982.

Towner, Wayne Sibley. *Genesis*. Westminster Bible Companion. Louisville, KY: Westminster John Knox Press, 2001.

von Rad, Gerhard. *Genesis: A Commentary*. Philadelphia: Westminster Press, 1973.

### Bible Study Aids

Achtemeier, Paul J., gen. ed. *The HarperCollins Bible Dictionary*. San Francisco: HarperCollins Publishers in consultation with the Society of Biblical Literature, 1996.

Frank, Harry Thomas, ed. *Atlas of the Bible Lands*. New ed. Union, NJ: Hammond World Atlas Corp., 2007.

Mays, James L., gen. ed. *The HarperCollins Bible Commentary*. San Francisco: HarperCollins Publishers in consultation with the Society of Biblical Literature, 2000.

*Nelson's Complete Book of Bible Maps and Charts*. Nashville: Thomas Nelson Publishers, 1996.

### Study Bibles

*The Discipleship Study Bible (NRSV) with Apocrypha*. Louisville, KY: Westminster John Knox Press, 2008. 2,197 pages.

> Features include introductory articles for each book of the Bible, study notes for key portions of each chapter of the Bible, a concise concordance, and helpful maps.

*The New Interpreter's Study Bible (NRSV) with Apocrypha.* Nashville: Abingdon Press, 2003. 2,298 pages.

> Features include introductory articles for each book of the Bible, extensive textual notes, many excursus essays, a helpful glossary, general articles related to biblical authority and interpretation, and colorful maps.

*The Access Bible (NRSV).* New York: Oxford University Press, 1999. 1,753 pages.

> Features include introductory articles for each book of the Bible; sidebar essays, maps, and charts in places appropriate to the text; section-by-section commentaries on the text; a glossary; a brief concordance; and a section of Bible maps in color.

*The NIV Study Bible.* Grand Rapids: Zondervan, 1985. 2,148 pages.

> Features include introductory articles and outlines for each book of the Bible; extensive notes for explanation and interpretation of the biblical text on each page; helpful charts, maps, and diagrams within the biblical text; an index to subjects; a concise concordance; and a collection of maps in color.

*The Learning Bible (CEV).* New York: American Bible Society, 2000. 2,391 pages.

> Features include introductory articles and outlines for each book of the Bible; fifteen background articles and over one hundred miniarticles; charts and timelines; a miniatlas; notes on biblical texts in six categories, each identified by a different color and symbol (geography; people and nations; objects, plants, and animals; ideas and concepts; history and culture; and cross-references); and hundreds of illustrations, photographs, and diagrams in color.